LESSONS FROM A
CLOWN

Paperback ISBN: 978-1-7399730-0-1

eBook ISBN: 978-1-7399730-1-8

LESSONS FROM A CLOWN

HOW TO FIND COURAGE TO SHOW UP FOR YOURSELF AND LAUGH EVERY DAY

EMMA STROUD

with

ORANGE

DEDICATION

for my dad and for William

Emma can move mountains with an infectious energy of joyful laughter and deep wisdom. Her life and work are an expression of hard-earned lessons in honouring your calling and living authentically. Spending time with her will inspire you to conquer your demons and make your mark in whatever way is truly right for you.

Dr. Amina Aitsi-Selmi ~ Founder and Managing Director,
Next Generation Coaching and Consulting,
author of *The Success Trap*

In […] Em's book – love, humanness, courage, lightness, humour, warmth, authenticity and realness are the ingredients that guide and drive Em to live a joyful life. The profound and innocent wisdom of Orange, an expanded part of Em, teaches us all to embrace the joy of life by enjoying the 'fruits' of being in touch with and allowing all of our to parts to show up and express in our life. Orange's loving letters to Em moved me so that I wept.

Pam Altaffer ~ Psychotherapist at Loving Your Relationships

One of my favourite things about Em is her ability to bring lightness and laughter to the often oh-too-serious endeavour of personal development. I'll admit to being prone to taking it all too seriously at times and Em's work (or is it play?) has shown me that it's possible, nay beneficial, to have a sense of humour about it all. Joy, laughter, and play are as important in doing deep work as anything else. *Lessons from a Clown* can teach us all how to be more comfortable in our own skin.

Vix Anderton ~ Founder and CEO, The Practical Balance

Em is a breath of fresh air 'on a mission to make the world laugh, think and play more!!' - what's not to love?! Taking her place in the noble line of clowns through the ages, ftom Shakespeare's fools to Hollywood's Robin Williams, Em will provoke, entertain and enquire....all with a good dose of fruit salad...

Harriet Beveridge ~ Coach, Comic, Co-author, *A Joosr Guide to... Will It Make the Boat Go Faster? by Ben Hunt-Davis and Harriet Beveridge: Olympic-Winning Strategies for Everyday Success*

Em just has a magic and unique way to get you thinking about things that could really change your life. For me the words Em and Play are synonymous. Everything she delivers is hilarious and joyful but also packed full of meaning and depth. If she writes it, you can bet that I am reading it as I know that its impact will be profound!

Jamie Brockehurst ~ Creator, *Where's My Lemonade?*

This book is a gift. Em reminds us in her incredibly generous and wonderfully warm way, that we each have more to live and enjoy. It resonates to the core. She presents us with priceless tools to unearth our selves. And through her raw and real tales, she leads us there so safely. Knowing Emma as a coach now for many years, I could not wait for this to be published. I know all too well how Emma time is like nectar for the soul and this is a whole book's worth!

Julie Cohen ~ Founder and CEO, Across the Pond agency

It's a big deal to be a Clown. So it takes a certain kind of heroine to let us into the captivating world of her Clown(s). This book dares to hold open spaces other people feel uncomfortable looking at. Em Stroud's insights are as bold as they are tender; the membrane between these is pretty thin. Not everyone's story gets to be tied up neatly with a bow at the end. And isn't that just the biggest gift of this book?

Danusia Malina Derben ~ Author, Podcaster, Coach

This is not the book for you if you want to become a clown. It is the book for you if you want to learn how to be more confident and present. Em is your genial guide through Clowndom and breaks down how Clowning can help us quash our egos, speak up for ourselves, and start enjoying our lives like we did when we were younger. I feel lucky to be in the same fruit salad as Em!

Clay Drinko, PhD ~ Author, *Play Your Way Sane*

What can I say about working with you that others won't say in a much better way. I guess the first thing is that you were the first person who enabled me to understand that all my past experiences that I had put into boxes didn't need to be opened, analysed over and over for me to move forward. All I had to do was accept that they were there, that they had made me who I was today. Then the next thing that you did for me was persuade me that I could accept compliments and believe them and that I might actually be an ok person who could do the job and that people did like. All of this enabled me to move forward with my own personal development but for me the real kicker was that it freed me up emotionally and intellectually to really help my team. To me you are a shining light of honesty, energy, knowledge and love.

Niki Fuchs ~ Managing Director, Office Space in Town

Emma is a one-of-a-kind. It is rare to find someone who can so instantly put you – or an audience of thousands, for that matter – at ease. She's funny, warm, wise and brings unique value to any project.

Hazel Gale ~ Therapist, Social Entrepreneur and Author, *The Mind Monster Solution*

[*Lessons from a Clown*] is for anyone who thinks that you can't play and get serious work done. And for people who know that play enhances serious work and creativity. It's also for people who want to enrich their lives with kindness. This book, in its exhortation to kindness and the practical - and gratifyingly impractical - tips on expanding playfulness, isn't for everyone. It's only for people who are willing to be sweetly challenged, for leaders who want to take a slo-mo, quantum leap in efficacy, and for people who are dead curious about this clown thing. Em Stroud is part of a tradition thousands of years in the running – leading from the front whilst seeming to be on the sidelines, with kindness and play, and sharing truths that otherwise might be too harsh to receive. You think you can't play and get serious work done? Nope. You think great leadership and play live on two separate continents? Nope. They not only live on the same street, but in the same house. You think you have outgrown your need to play? Absolutely not. Em Stroud, with immense courage and kindness, exhorts you to bravely join, and bring your wonder to, the fabulous, poignant, marvellous party of life and work.

Dr. Shoshana Garfield ~ Leadership Coach, Speaker, Torture Recovery Expert, and Author, *The Smart Person's Guide to Big Fat Lies About Suffering Stress and Happiness*

If only we all had Orange in our lives – the world would feel a better place. This book opened my eyes to what a clown is and expanded my mind. Written in a frank, engaging and humorous manner the book shines a light on Orange (Emma's clown) and also the clown that is within us all. Expect metaphors, fruit salad and heartfelt tears with a sense of depth, honesty and authenticity ... and that is just from the first chapter.

Joanna Gilbert ~ Artist

Emma is a torrent of fresh air. Innovative, witty, engaging and authentic. She reminds us all to stay in touch with our inner clown.

Samantha Grierson ~ Writer and Director, Samantha Grierson Media Ltd

---

The energy in this book is off the charts! From the author's clownful cheerleading to simple things like the break-the-snoozy-norm layout, you feel empowered to be crazy and authentic and bold, right out of the gate. I've read so many self-help books, but there's something uniquely powerful about one written from the perspective of someone that has found a way to intersect two seemingly polar opposites - their inner-passion (being a bona fide Clown!) with business (coaching, speaking). The author's unique experience and coaching make it feel like you can literally design a recipe for work, life and success in ANY way you want!

Erin Hatzikostas, ~ Author, *You Do You(ish)*

Early on in *Lessons From a Clown*, Em explains that we shouldn't be scared of clowns as there is a great deal of clown misinformation out there and it's all fake news. Which was heartening. As someone with claustrophobic tendencies, I have been kept awake many a night wondering how so many fit into one small car, especially in those oversized shoes? But this book is the opposite of claustrophobic, it instead gives you the tools to breathe through life. Em explains that clowns are not the enemy, but our own thoughts can be. She writes in an ever evolving, upbeat stream of articulate consciousness, talking to you, not at you. Em knows how to ask questions whilst making you feel positive about the answers, whatever they may be. If you want to take more positivity into work, life, relationships or just your own mind then *Lessons from a Clown* is for you.

James Kermack ~ Writer, Director, Actor, films Knuckledust and Hi-Lo Joe

---

Emma puts into *Lessons from a Clown* the simple, yet extremely difficult, hope for us all – how to have more fun and be ourselves in everything we do and say each minute of each great day. [...] I have seen the effect her work has on the most professional and serious business people and the way it has transformed their presence in/around their businesses and lives – inspirational. By putting very delicate and serious work into the mind of a clown is brilliant and the realisation that fun and laughter really make the world go around is certain to get you to a wider more fulfilled place – a book to hold by your heart each day!!

Paul Knee ~ PFK Business Coaching Limited

Only Emma Stroud can pull off a book that's both urgent and spit-out-your-tea funny. In a heavy world, her levity is a balm. By weaving in her own wonky path to the human she's become, Stroud will help many to recognise themselves – maybe for the first time, as a refreshing "fruit salad." Fun-spirational.

Dr. Mandy Lehto ~ Coach, Speaker, Writer, and Champion of high achievers, and Host of "Enough The Podcast"

For all of us finding our true selves is a life's work, it's exposing, it's scary, it's often alarming, and if you want to survive the process laughter is your safety net. To then find the courage to put that discovery down on paper for the world (hopefully) to read is a whole other level of bravery. To put it down on paper in a way that can help others do the same, is a whole other level of cleverness.

Annemarie Lewis Thomas ~ Principal/CEO, Musical Theatre Academy

---

I am fascinated by the idea that each of us has an inner clown waiting to be discovered. I've been introduced to the world of clowning a few times now. It seems to keep knocking at my door, inviting me to play. I think Em's book *Lessons from a Clown* will provide me and others with rich insight and ways to do this, by sharing her stories and encouraging our curiosity, creativity and courage to go forth and discover our own inner clowns …Thanks Em for continuing to shine a light on you, your work and the clowns that make you who you are. Keep on clowning …

Dr. Cathryn Lloyd ~ Founder/Director, Facilitator and Creativity Coach at Maverick Minds and Seriously Playful Creativity

---

Em Stroud is a shining light of silliness and joy, fuelled by real intelligence and passion. This book is living proof that it is never too late for you to discover the best version of yourself.

Tom Mayhew ~ Stand Up Comic

Emma takes you on a joyful journey with her Clown, Orange. And quite frankly, Orange is the only kind of leader we should follow as we struggle to navigate these turbulent times. She's brutally authentic and draws her wisdom from the present moment. This book is a must read for anyone who wants to stop floundering about and is finally ready to show up in their life and career as who they truly are.

Miisa Mink ~ Founder and Chief Doer, DrivenWoman

Clowning around is what Emma was born to do. But this really is no joke. Her work is as insightful as it is fun and she brings out that inner creativity in all of us that is so often locked away. Always a pleasure to be around and someone who is as passionate about how she makes people feel as she is about her profession. Stay Boom! Emma.

Scott Morrison ~ Founder and Bringer of the Boom!

Em has brought me such deep insights into humanity and therefore my own being. [...] The depth of authenticity Em brings is from the heart. She opens up courageously and mere words on a page become intensely important and invite us in with empathy ... she guides you on tales of wonder and curiosity that urge you to explore your own thoughts and feelings and humanity with an accomplished authorial ease. This is genius storytelling.

Stuart Packer ~ Actor, Storyteller, Storytelling Coach, Facilitator

---

Your book is amazing. Truly amazing. I could use a lot of words to say why this is the case but there are three that keep springing to mind. Your book will help your readers: BE. MORE. HUMAN. In reading it I am reminded to allow the kind part of myself to come out and play; to have a voice and to grab the steering wheel of this thing called life and point it in the direction of the light. As a campaigner on a mission of inspiring the creation of a mentally healthier world, this feels important. Thank you for sharing your soul by introducing us to Orange and for inspiring us all to connect with our inner clown as we could all do with more self kindness during these times.

Rob Stephenson ~ Founder and CEO, FormScore

Emma captures perfectly the importance of embracing your alter ego and living your life to full, live, laugh, clown around, what's not to love!

Vanessa Vallely, OBE ~ Founder of We Are The City, and Author, *Heels of Steel*

"The role of a clown and a physician are the same – to elevate the possible and to relieve suffering."

Robin Williams,
in the role of Hunter "Patch" Adams in the 1998 film, "Patch Adams"

TABLE OF CONTENTS

PART ONE

THE OPENER

'So, what do you do?' asks an attractive woman I've met for a dinner date. I look at her and take the plunge.

'I am a Clown.'

Her eyebrows go up. 'Really?' she says, 'an actual Clown?'

'Yip. An actual Clown.' It is the first time I've owned this part of me while out on a date and this feels especially brave here, even a little reckless. In the past I would have said podcaster or coach, improviser or speaker to describe what I do, as these are (said in my full British accent) "proper things", acceptable, known. But I am being courageous in a way that I've been learning from Orange, my Clown.

The woman across the table is still looking at me with a quizzical eye, and says, 'Tell me more.' I inhale and begin.

So I am doing this. I am owning being a Clown, here in my personal life. Fuck it. I want to be me. If she wants to know ***me*** *she will have to know* ***all of me.***

We chat. One year later she is my girlfriend.

Being a Clown is the best part of me. Clowning changed me for the better. This is what I have been taught so far....

FADE IN:

EM STROUD enters a small and intimate space. The audience is there waiting in anticipation. EM is dressed in a black top, black trousers and wears red DC trainers. She goes to the mic and takes it off the too high stand.

EM

You're doing pretty much okay in your life, right now! In some ways you're actually doing pretty well. Whoop! Whoop! I mean, outwardly you're ticking all the grown-up boxes. Well done! You've got the job. You may or may not have a partner, and if you don't, you're probably actively dating and savouring how you're the envy of your married friends who all miss being single. (Well, they don't miss *being* single exactly … Of course, all you married and partnered-up people are *really* happy, aren't you? Yes, of course you are!! But still, you do quite enjoy living vicariously through your single friends, don't you? Hearing their stories makes you feel like you're alive and helps you believe that your life can still evolve and change. (Have I got that about right?) Fingers crossed!

Yet … 'Is this it?' often floats in your mind as you look around your lovely house with your lovely partner, oh, and now a charming dog. And you singles hear, 'Will I ever find the right one?' You're wondering if it's possible. And let's not even mention the thought of children. I mean, will you ever have them? Then again, do you want them? Ah … life and its complexities!!

And I mean, look at you! You've got a fabulous group of friends, even if you don't get to see them enough, as alas, you're always working. Or doing something else, as your life is **very busy**, always so **very busy**.

Yet, you're not entirely sure how it ended up this way, are you? Something doesn't feel quite right, does it? What is it, though? You have no idea. And let's be honest, you have not got the time to really think about it as you are so **very busy** – being, well, **busy**. You know that if you only had the courage to say the things you want to say, and if that stupid, incessant, little inner voice would be quiet instead of telling you that you are too loud, too bossy, and too quiet, hell, why not, let's go there, and – too not enough – then maybe, just maybe, your life could be a bit different. A bit better. Nothing dramatic has to really happen in order for that to be true. You just need a little time, where you can check in with you. Ahhh, but you're too busy for that, aren't you? And let's face this too, if you actually let yourself do that, take the time and check in, then stuff might *actually* change. And who wants that, right? Who really wants deep happiness or living fully, and to your own potential while doing what makes their heart sing? I mean, who actually wants that when you are doing just fine, afterall, pretty well, and thanks for asking. I mean who possibly wants to laugh more?

Right?

I get it. I've been there. For me, there came a moment when being just fine and doing pretty well to the rest of the world wasn't enough anymore. I remember the moment when I knew something wasn't right, when I realised there was more to life, that life was too short to live like that. I didn't want to be looking back in ten years' time and saying I wasted my 40s. I had no idea it was going to take the art of clowning to teach me the simple lessons of what life is really about – but it did and I'm grateful.

Are you ready to move away from being fine?

I'm thinking you are.

Great.

Let's get started.

EM leaves the stage putting the microphone back on the still too high mic stand. EM smiles at the audience and they get up for their drinks break.

WHAT IS A CLOWN, REALLY?

When I tell people I'm a Clown I get the following reactions:

- A wide-eyed, hand-over-the-mouth look of fear. It's possible they are terrified of or even phobic about Clowns. I feel sad for these folks, because somewhere along the way they got the wrong message about Clowns, just like I had about snakes. I blame Mrs Allan for that fear, after she unexpectedly put an old snakeskin on my head when I was 9-years-old! (Don't worry though. I've had hypnotherapy so I can now look at snakes on TV – Go me!!)
- A deeply concerned face followed by a question resembling this: 'Clowns and business don't really mix, do they?' (Generally fuelled by the aforementioned fear.)
- Blurted clarifying questions like: 'Well then where's your red nose, tiny bicycle, big shoes …' (You get the idea.)
- Offhanded, mildly insulting remarks which typically include: 'So, you do kids parties then?' (Uh, no. No, I don't do parties. Although if I did, they really would be magical, and the kids would love them.)
- And, ever so occasionally, I hear some curious truths, like 'Oh cool!' which are just as occasionally followed by admissions akin to, 'But I have no idea what a clown really is.'

I love this last response and as you've picked up *Lessons from A Clown*, I hope you're just as curious.

Clowning, and in particular my Clown, Orange has helped me be happier. I've been able to reconnect with who I am and harness my courage, and I definitely laugh more. I'm going to share here what I've learned from exploring and being in the Clowning world. I am not suggesting that you should go and take Clowning courses or even that you need to venture near that part of my world. I'm offering to you, gleaned from over twenty years of working in business as a coach, speaker, and trainer as well performing in shows all across the UK, what I believe all of us can learn from the wonders, craft and skills of Clowning.

Embracing these lessons has enabled me to deepen my sense of purpose, and my way of being in the world. I've learned to trust that laughter and play are as vital to us now as they have always been, but we've strayed from understanding how much we need them. I spent a nearly twenty years – (I know I am shocked too as it feels that I am still about five) exploring the world of improvisation in business and have done thousands of talks and workshops on this. Yet I hadn't made the link between Clowning and my body of work until about three years ago when I started exploring Clowning anew. That feeling of truly showing up as myself in the world – one I'd sought my entire life – is something that Clowning made possible for me. It connected all of my worlds, all of the parts of myself, and I wrote *Lessons from a Clown* to enable you to feel this in your life too.

This is not a workbook, a coaching manifesto, or a memoir. It is none of these, yet all of these. I mean, when I'm already putting myself out there as a Clown, which induces the responses I listed earlier, why would I write a book that a traditional label can be applied to, right?

Not writing one of these types of books is a conscious choice, because it was important that anything I write suit me. I've never felt I fit neatly into one box, and I have struggled with people trying to put me into just such a box – so, I wrote *Lessons from a Clown* with the intention of defying easy definition and rebelling against some limiting categories. I know my very clever marketing friends would say this is a cardinal error. They'd say that I must have clarity, be intentional, squarely land my book in a specific market ... but those fine people would be missing the point. Sure, I can suggest some personal development style tactics, as I'm schooled in the methods, processes, and modalities of that space. I can also be a coach at times. I am also a storyteller at heart – so expect stories aplenty!! (You have been are warned!) And face it, we all love stories – well at least good ones that make sense to you. I hope you'll read with an open heart, with curiosity, and a willingness to laugh at me, with yourself, and with me. This book and the heart of Clowning have enabled me to be all that I am, and I trust they can help you be all of you. (And yes, laugh more!!)

All right, all right, I can hear you from here: 'But, Em how will this actually, you know, make me like my life better?' On to the good stuff – what this book will do for you.

[WARNING! ALERT! ALERT!
I AM GOING TO GET QUITE DEEP ...]

KNOW WHO YOU ARE

I understand that you outwardly know what you are capable of, and no doubt you link who you are to what you do. This is fab. However, I wonder what difference it would make to you if you got to spend some time thinking about who you are away from your work?

What makes you tick?

What's super important to you?

What makes your heart sing?

Why are you not allowing yourself to do more of those things?

[STILL IN THE DEEP CONTENT HERE, STAY WITH ME ...]

GROW A TRUE SENSE OF CONFIDENCE

So many people I have worked with say, 'Em, I want to be more confident.' These lessons will help you realise that confidence on its own is given too much power as a word. We will explore how you can feel more confident by understanding and knowing yourself, and I'll suggest other things for you to think about, rather than listening to the "I-am-not-confident" inner voice that so many of us struggle to ignore.

[Aside – Everyone has challenges with this – from Global CEOs to prominent famous people – all of them. (And I know as I have worked with them.) They all have that inner voice. The good news is that there is so much we can all do to change it. Whoop! Whoop!]

SHOW UP AS ALL OF YOU, ALWAYS

So, you can put the masks away. Time and time again people tell me they are really different at home compared to how they are at work. One woman told me she was literally Jekyll and Hyde (not in a scary way, I hasten to add.) At work she felt she had to be the type of soul who spoke up, and be very clear in her leadership, while at home she was just quiet and gentle. No one wins in this scenario. I want to present you with the freedom to choose how you want to show up in any situation, to be all of you, and the best of you, always.

BE MORE CURIOUS

About yourself. Too many of us make decisions in our 20s that then dictate the rest of our lives. We stop seeking. We quite often stop learning because we're too busy being busy and living our lives. By adding more curiosity into your life and heart, you'll feel more expansive and become more joyous. You'll feel happier, and who doesn't want that? I mean, what's not to love about that?

OPEN UP TO YOUR CREATIVITY

Now, I know some of you will read this and say, 'But I'm not creative.' To those folks I say: Yes. You. Are. Your creativity may be hidden, or you might be blocked because of a belief you have from your past. For all of us, even if you do feel you're creative, there is always room to be more so. Be more open. It will make you better at problem-solving, more fun to work with, a better parent, and a better partner – all in all a better human!! Whoop! Whoop! And you are already brilliant, so win-win!

LAUGH MORE

Let's face it, none of us are laughing enough. Up until the age of 23 we laugh 300 times a day. After this age it becomes 300 times a month. Scary and true – this comes from *Humour Seriously*, a fab book all about how we can all use more humour in our worlds. This lack is why I have founded laughthinkplay.com. We all know how great it is to laugh, yet we don't allow ourselves to do enough of it. It's quite bonkers, right?

HAVE MORE FUN

Fun is good. The manner in which we understand fun will be different for each of us. Hand on heart here, friends: Are you having enough fun? (I know you aren't.) Yet, how great does it feel right now knowing that's about to change? Go on, deny that little feeling in your tummy, if you dare. ☺

If all of this appeals, read on. If not, then put this book down immediately and avoid it like the plague. I mean, *who wants to have more fun, hey?*

I do understand the challenges of accepting having more fun, *as an idea*. I've worked with thousands of people and I'm still shocked by how many of us find play and fun are frightening concepts. I think we're afraid of getting it wrong, or even worse, of looking silly. There is also the internal pressure to "being funny". There are so many self-critical labels we attach to ourselves when we're not being serious, or acting as we think we're expected to, particularly at work. What I have learnt and seen is that when you allow yourself to play, relax, and have more fun, people follow you. There is a freedom in being in touch with these parts of yourself. I am not suggesting that every meeting you go to or every interaction should have humour in it. What I *am* suggesting is that there can be a lighter approach, one where we take the pressure off and allow ourselves to be the best of us and find joy through fun and play.

We used to know exactly how to do this.

Let's just go to a nursery for a moment. Picture the scene with twenty little people all moving about. Have a look around … there are kids

playing in the sand

building stuff

creating imaginary games

drawing

pushing cars around

running

looking at books.

… and (fill in the gaps here for yourself).

At that age there are no restrictions, we just play … and at one point in your life, you were one of these kids. So, the way you have fun or play would likely be different from what I do for fun or play. Makes sense, right?

We all bring our own uniqueness to the world.

That's right, you. You are unique and the world needs you to be you.

At a recent speaking gig I asked everyone: 'What does play feel like for you and how does it show up in your life?' All the answers were different. Some were surprising. Throughout this book I will be making suggestions and encouraging you to do what works for you and ignore what doesn't and this is why.

The individuality of fun and play was really important for me to accept. Once I allowed myself to understand that how we all have fun is different, everything started to make sense. Like the feeling of finally finishing a puzzle. (I'm terrible at puzzles so this really is a win when I finish one.) I became better able to help others find their joy. It is my job here to help you *allow* yourself to *remind* yourself that fun, laughter, joy, and play are good for you, and when you do that, you will have a greater impact in whatever world you find yourself in right now.

I once did a talk to a room of CEOs. In the client's advance instructions to me it stated clearly that I was to do all my stuff, but that there would definitely *not* be any game playing. The CEOs would not get the idea of games. The client who was booking me considered them time-consuming and costly to productivity. I said, 'Yes, of course' knowing in the back of my mind there would *definitely* be games. (I do I hasten to add, pay attention to briefs when they are correct – yet I think people who are dealing with senior professionals sometimes forget that they are human too!) Ten minutes or so into the gig, after sharing success stories as a group we started to play games. Were they out of their comfort zone? Yip! Did they giggle and laugh, and then learn? Yip!

I got some of the best feedback ever from that group, including comments about how being encouraged to be open and playing had made it possible for them to reconnect with parts of themselves they had forgotten about.

Lessons from a Clown will give you all the tools you need in order to recapture your essence -- and yes, your inner child, as well as much more.

For me, my Clowns (I have three, thus far) allow me access the different parts of me that I would be too scared to explore and expose to the world otherwise.

Nina Levine says it this way:

> *Clowning necessitates a willingness to take risks and use failure as a springboard to the next moment. The process is observed through the clown's struggle to triumph over adversity. She thinks she is in control, but the audience clearly sees she is not. The fun is in the discrepancy. Theatrical clowning emphasises character and relationships rather*

> *than circus skills. Material is created by conceptualization and improvisation, often utilizing one's own life experiences, though not strictly autobiographical. Therefore, the audience is witness to a personal portrait of human folly. My approach to the character and circumstances is not unlike that of a traditional acting role, drawing on technique, intention and obstacles. It is also physical, employing at times pratfalls, slapstick, and dance. I refer to clowning as "brilliant stupidity".*[1]

My Clowns and I want you to think of us in the context of theatre clowns. If this doesn't ring any bells for you, then think of the Shakespearean Fool, or the Court Jester – the observers of life. We watch, and then say what we see. We can say things that others would hesitate to, using humour as the interface with their discomfort.

We are the truth tellers and the mood changers. We always arrive with the intention of serving others.

In my view, Clowns come from a place of no ego – willing to acknowledge that everyone else around us knows more than we do. In theatrical terms the audience will always know more than me, the Clown. This does not mean that Clowns are not smart. Neither does it mean that Clowns are always "good" characters. There are moody, grumpy, and in some cases even angry Clowns. However, these are very conscious states that the Clown has chosen to play with, and from those postures and those emotional states that they can engage with the audience. But they are still truth tellers. They are still present. And they still will, in their own way, bring joy to the world.

Clowns reflect all of us as humans.

Clowns play with the truth and have the freedom to explore.

Clowns bring us so much, yet sadly, like most things that have good intentions, they can be misinterpreted and misunderstood. For me, being a Clown enables me to be the most human I can be. There have been

Clowns throughout the world since we have records of us as humans. Clowns come in many different forms, such as buffoon, mime, and whiteface. In modern day most people think of Clowns based on the recognisable Auguste or red clown type – the big costumes, big shoes and wearing lots of colour. These Clowns entertain large audiences and developed from the 1860s, later leading to Clowns being used as kids entertainers and eventually showing up in films portraying them as evil. These Clowns came out of circus and vaudeville and across the world they had many evolutions. The harlequin clown, developed and used a lot within British pantomime in the 17th century, is one many people think of. The Clown was present in Greek and Roman theatre, and the style that developed in Italy as part of Commedia dell'arte actually influenced early British pantomime. Clowns can vary from Charlie Chaplin, to Sascha Baron Cohen, to Caroline Aherne as Mrs Merton. Throughout time they have served a socio-religious or psychological role – as Goffman, Mills and Berger write – "… it seems plausible that folly and fools, like religion and magic meet some deeply rooted needs in human society."[2]

Orange is part of a long tradition of Clowns.

Clowning allows us as performers to deal with challenging content. In my current show *Re:Framed*, Orange delivers the most harrowing lines. *Re:Framed* is autobiographical, and my intention with sharing the worst of my own past is to mirror hope for the audience. Using Orange as the vehicle to deliver these lines enables me as the performer to explore uncomfortable content within the script and challenge the audience while Orange's persona offers a foundation of safety and connection. In fact, Orange keeps *me* safe as well because Orange can utter lines containing bluntly-worded truths that would be "too much" for both me and the audience. (This is the joy of being a creative! I mean why not use all your own past and trauma to create a theatre show and film, right? Go me!!) With Orange playing the role of the observer and the truthteller the message is equally profound yet offered almost as a suggestion rather than a personal revelation which it would appear to be if I said as myself. The audience is safer because they are being captivated by the wonderment that Orange exudes, and I am safer because I do not have to relive the experience, or the feelings of the story Orange is telling.

For a long time, I thought that everyone lived in a similar manner to me. As I hit the 40-year mark I realised that perhaps this was not the case ... one example of this is that I have a weird fruit narrative. (Stay with me here!) Yes, I did my TEDx talk dressed as a banana but in actuality my fruit thought process runs much deeper than just that. (Surely, all of us think of ourselves as fruit, right?)

FRUIT SALAD

One of the purposes I felt strongly about in drafting *Lessons From A Clown* was to support a better translation of the art of and lessons from Clowning to the non-Clowning world. As humans we like to stay with our own, maybe because this makes sense to us, yet this has never been my way of living. I am at heart super curious (not nosey, there is a difference people!). This curiosity has led me to stand in many different rooms with so many different types of people – who are all very driven in their own worlds. I am driven yes, but I am driven by seeking how I can be the best of me. When I enter a room I ask myself: What can I learn from all these different brilliant people? And also, how do I fit in here (or do I fit in)?

This has led me to see the world as a fruit salad …

[**WARNING – INSIGHT ALERT!**

LAUGHING AND A LIGHTNESS OF TOUCH WILL MAKE YOU HAPPIER – TRUE!!]

I have long used the metaphor of a fruit bowl to illustrate how I believe each of us makes choices about how we show up in the world. (Yip, you read that right. I said fruit bowl. I mean, you're reading a book written by a Clown … so you should expect some metaphors that make you raise your eyebrows. Stay with me, here …)

Some of us are a fruit salad, made up of all of the different fruits we are. For me it looks like this:

Bananas – clowns

Strawberries – improvisers

Blueberries – entrepreneurs

Apples – business folk

Melons – mums

Raspberries – other speakers

Grapes – other gay folk

Pears – coaches

Kiwis – other podcasters and radio folk

I love being the full fruit bowl and I can go and play with any of these fruits (and more!) – but if I spend too long only being one, I start to feel I'm not enjoying myself as much. I need the variety. I need to be able to move from one fruit to the other – this fuels me. It took me a while to acknowledge this about myself, but I was so much happier once I did.

All the fruits and the whole bowl make up me. When I am working with one-to-one coaching clients, I can quite often be found bringing a game into a session and my Clown will make an appearance when needed. Same as when I am speaking, I can't help but use the tools of improvising in my speaking gigs. These different fruits and having the confidence to be all of them is really freeing. It has enabled me to get to a point in my life where I *really* give a shit, but I also don't give a shit at all.

Don't follow me? Read on.

I took a look at my diary today and was reminded yet again how accurate the fruit bowl metaphor is for me.

I'm making a film trailer,

doing workshops,

leading online speaking gigs and

coaching some one-to-one clients.

I'm seeing some friends,

hosting William's 9th Birthday (how is he 9?!!) and

hanging out with my girlfriend.

I'm attending a meeting with the school,

recording a few podcast episodes and

keeping up with my email mates.

You get the gist!

I was feeling grateful that I have all these different elements to my week – then I caught myself smiling. I could see that I was doing the work I love to do, and that I was fully engaged in each of these interactions, fully into what I was meant to be doing, because I'm being all the fruits!!

This reframing of my life through the lens of my diary has helped me get to the point that I no longer worry about what people think of me. I'm only concerned with being the best Em I can be. My job is to really be fully with all these people and then move on to the next person or group. This freedom of really giving a shit but not giving a shit has enabled me to do the best work of my life – but more than that it has allowed me to be me.

Lots of brilliant people I know are very happy to be one fruit for the majority of time - one my clients is a super successful business woman – she spends her life on her business and then for six weeks of the year just switches off and is with her family. She is content. She is secure in her choices and loves that she is clear on what she is doing. She knows what her fruits are and how they make her happy.

Joanna Gilbert (a brilliant artist!) who I interviewed on my Clowning Around podcast has three distinct fruits – her art fruit, her marketing fruit and her mother fruit. Now she may not have thought of it in fruit terms – but what she has done is be become super clear in the conscious choices she makes in her life.

I have a really good friend who is a teacher and a mum. She is quite possibly one of the happiest souls I know! She is so content in living as both of these fruits that she has no desire for any other – what she has done is become super conscious that these are her choices, and as such her life is going brilliantly. I recall working with someone once who was trying to juggle being many fruits as that was what he thought success looked like. When we worked together it became clear that all he really wanted to be was a storyteller and this clarity changed the direction of his life when he chose to focus on that one part of himself. He directed his attention, time and energy to *his* fruit, and he is now so happy.

Are you one fruit, two fruits or three fruits? More? (Hoping you are now thinking of the song!)

What feels great for you?

Own the fruit! Own your life! Laugh more! I mean bananas are just always funny and how can you not enjoy life a bit more if you think of your life as a blueberry? ☺

Are you proudly one fruit who likes to hang out with the same kind of fruit all the time? Or are you made up of many fruits, and a bit of a fruit salad like me?

Or did you used to be a full fruit bowl and gradually life has left you feeling like you can only be one type, say, a blueberry? If that is the case the lessons in this book will help you rediscover your other fruits and how you can fully inhabit them.

LESSONS

I mean that's quite an intense word from a Clown ... how will these so-called lessons really help me? I mean like really help me? (I can hear you asking.)

I get that knowing yourself better can be scary territory. It is easier to stay busy instead, isn't it? It is easier to carry on living, never stopping, always moving, never getting into the vulnerability of the unknown, the curiosity, the asking for more, for wanting more for you, so that you can live the best human life you can. You know you deserve that, right?

Clowns are inherently human. My clowns and Orange tap into my humanity, the fullness of me perhaps more than anything else I do.

As Mark Lonergan states: "The greatest clowns are, while acting in a foolish or silly manner, very honest performers. Good clowns reveal something very truthful about themselves. And that's one of the things that makes clowning so incredibly difficult. It's a very vulnerable place to be in as a performer. There are a lot of people who try it and give up because they find it too scary or challenging. There are very few people who can do it really well."[3]

It is this honesty that helps people relate to clowns. Samantha Holdsworth runs the UK arm of the global organisation Clowning Without Borders (https://www.cwb-international.org/) the purpose of which is to bring joy and light into refugee camps. The organisation's original aim as I understand it was to work with the kids – to show them some light. Yet it became evident over time that the work that these Clowns were doing would be just as important for the adults. She joined me on my podcast – she is great, have a listen.

Clowning and the doors that Clowns can open allow us to see and feel the light that always exists – this "light" that I refer to is the spark that makes each of us who we are. It is that thing you can't name but can't help seeing the moment you witness someone talking about something they love. Their face changes and you can feel how engaged their energy is. This is not about achievement or success – this light is the part of us that activates when we connect with it. Others can't fail to see it, feel it, or hear it. It's the part of you that makes you feel the most alive. I believe all of us have a light inside us. During times I've most despaired in my life, ironically my struggle has been almost imperceptible to me as well as to others. But I have always recognised its presence. Eventually.

I have watched us go through our mental health challenges and endure the collective grief that is COVID-19 as I write, witnessing across the world (from my living room – thanks, COVID lockdown) how the pandemic has caused us all to open up more in business, to more deeply embrace our humanity. We have opened our homes to people we work with, and we have become nonchalant about kids and pets interrupting us. We all understand. This is what the lessons can help us do – be more human and understand ourselves and each other better.

When I think of all of us and the challenges we face as a species I can get massively overwhelmed, akin to news fatigue. You need only look at the media and you can believe that there is no good in the world, that only negative events are happening right now. Of course, I understand that there are some awful life-changing events happening daily – in no way do I want to minimise them. Yet, if we allow ourselves to focus on what we can control then we can change the world and get through this crisis and emerge perhaps better than when we went into it – that's a good thought, right?

HOW DID I GET HERE? (I ASK MYSELF THAT A LOT!) AND HOW WILL THIS HELP YOU?

At its heart my work seeks to help people live happier, more impactful lives as I show up in my myriad roles – speaker, coach, trainer, performer or podcaster, each of which I've sought as a bridge to help people evolve to be the best version of themselves. Reconnecting with Clowning made me realise that the only one I can change, and the only person I'm in charge of, is me. We spend so much of our energy and time focusing on others – their perceptions, and their judgements. For many of us, who we decide to be and how we choose to behave is directed related to what we think will make us appear "successful".

Fifteen years ago, I set up a theatre company. We had some successful performances around the UK. We also grew the side of the business that would work with other businesses including engineering firms, tech companies and communication companies. As the business side of the theatre company grew, I found myself moving more and more away from my performing side. I started to mask up, thinking that people in business would not take me seriously if they knew I performed. I began to lose myself.

I have always feared appearing to everyone as all of me. I have been mired in the worry that I would be rejected and feel abandoned or deeply unlovable as I did in my early life. Masking, and making others laugh became my modus operandi in my professional life until a few years ago. I had set up the theatre company so I could be "in charge", be in control, and be the leader. I found it so much easier to be the leader and hold space for people than be a participant. Sound familiar at all?

I grew up in what as outwardly the "perfect" household and family, in the rolling hills of the Surrey countryside in the UK, including attending the private all-girls school. The reality of my childhood was far from perfect. My dad died when I was ten and sadly my mum was not able to see me as what I was then – a child looking for love. She and I became distant and survived in a house that was cold and unfeeling. I left the big yellow house when I was 17 and spent most of my early adult years avoiding and running from the effects of that time. I have not spoken to my mum now for over ten years. My upbringing and the beliefs I established in it dictated how I lived for nearly twenty years. Until I said no more.

To the rest of the world, I know that I have always appeared to be doing well, running businesses and putting myself "out there". Yet in my inner life I have felt flawed. I work with many people that have this feeling and who have been putting great effort into being unseen by others. As I say in my show *Re:Framed:*

Funny is a shield. How do people not see?

INTRODUCING ORANGE

Orange has taught me so much. Orange was always there within me and it's no coincidence that I am writing this book with Orange. Orange is the lightness of me. As I embrace putting my lessons into the world, my co-author had to be Orange as Orange taught me these lessons first.

Orange enables me to see things from a true perspective. Imagine that there is this part of you that is so free and expressive, that has unfettered permission to see the most wonderful things in the world. We all do have that. We all do have that part of us but it's fleeting, temporary, or short-term. When I inhabit Orange that wonderment is present for me all the time. It is also exhausting being Orange – because Orange misses nothing – it is the fullest experience of being present I've ever had.

Orange would not even want these words written about Orange as Orange is too in the moment, too in the now. In fact, as I ask Orange what Orange thinks Orange is telling me to look at the sunrise and reminding me that I have just missed it, because I'm too busy writing. Orange is my guide and observer into goodness. Into allowing. Into joy.

Orange has shifted me as much as hours of therapy have done. With Orange I could connect to the younger me that wanted to play; that same younger me that was perhaps not always allowed out. Orange is childlike; that part of me as a child that never got expressed, but that is a part of me still, plus a part that is all Orange of which I have no control over. Orange gives me the space and wonder to explore the world. As Orange even the same room can look completely different, if I let myself really look. Orange is the best friend that I never had. As Orange helps me see the world from a different, better perspective. Orange is that bit of you that you allow to show up for all your friends – you know the way you show up brilliantly, all full of advice for your friends but less so for yourself? You know the part! Orange asks me to look and really see who I am; not who I believed I was based upon other people's judgement.

Plus, Orange is a shit load of fun.

My voice is the one that you have heard so far, the one that is quite often a bit silly, reflecting a person whose life's purpose is to make the world laugh, think and play more. Orange will interrupt occasionally in future. If you listen to Clowning Around ... you'll know Barbara as well. She is set there and happy in that world. Orange is keen to be involved here. For those of you that are super at paying attention you'll recall that I said I had three clowns. The final clown is Frank. I know him the least so far – as when I was getting to know him at a Drag King workshop (yes, really!) our chances of getting to know Frank better disappeared because of COVID-19. What I do know is that he tries really hard and gets things wrong ... all the time!! To see how he develops follow me on social media.

I first met Orange in 2018 when I signed up to complete my first course with my teacher, the amazing Angela De Castro – who has performed around the world and shares her methodology to thousands of people through the Why Not Institute – or De Castro as we call her. De Castro is a Brazilian woman of diminutive stature like me – I think she is actually smaller than me and I stand at the great height of five foot two inches, so that is quite a rarity for me!! De Castro has a sharp intellect and can almost smell the truth of who you are. This is a gift that many teachers in the theatre world have – they are so used to seeking and finding truth for themselves that instinctively they can see you masking up. They spot it straight away. De Castro is one of the few people I can admit to being slightly scared of when I first met them. She is an amazing performer, teacher, director and one of the world's finest clowns. I had followed her work from afar for quite a few years and I always knew where she was teaching and when.

I was accepted into a course called How to be a Stupid. Just getting accepted was a buzz as I had not had to write a CV for years – so that was an interesting challenge! I think my cover letter got me a slot, as the course name alone provoked a reaction in me, and I played with the word stupid in that letter.

On a cold January day, I got myself to a church hall in South West London full of fear, adrenaline, and a whole load of curiosity. I was re–entering the world of Clowning. I had experienced Clowning while studying theatre and performing arts at university – not business studies as I was meant to do and as was expected of me. I followed my heart and as part of my degree we did one term of Clowning and Commedia dell'arte. I loved the masking, the hiding, and the wonder of what play could open up to me. I was seduced by the skill of Clowning – the part of the story of it that I wanted to own – that it could give me a place to hide.

At that point in my late teens I wasn't ready to fully embrace the story of my damaging childhood. I was terrified of my own image, and I couldn't even comprehend the idea of being gay, so I was pushing myself to sleep with men. I was desperately seeking love and solace in unhealthy worlds, and I'd been the victim of rape which I thought just confirmed how broken and unlovable I really was. I was caught up in my trauma and living the life of a student rebelling against the world. I moved from one avoidant tactic to another. All while looking to the world that I was "doing really well".

I travelled to Italy to learn more. Clowning and its inherent honesty had hooked me, but I was too fearful to explore that fully so as quickly as I had picked it up – I let it go again. A common pattern for me then.

Living in Devon after university I was lucky enough to meet some brilliant writers and theatre producers. One of them was an amazing playwright who is still my friend Natalie McGrath, who cast me in the John Osborne play "The Entertainer". I was the only non-professional actor, and not knowing I should do vocal warmups, I lost my voice on the second night. It was a clear indicator that I needed to go to drama school. I wanted to learn the craft of acting but my deeper personal yearning was to get really good at pretending. I wanted to carry on hiding, which for me at that time in my life meant pushing down all the hurt that I felt. I was burying a mass of vulnerabilities, of self-critical beliefs that I was a failure, a horrible person and destined to not amount to much, meanwhile outward appearances showed otherwise.

At the end of the first year of drama school I realised that acting is the portrayal of truth – and I had to confront this fact: To learn to act I had to face myself. I was going to have to be brave and look at all the stuff I'd been repressing and quit pretending. I had to make this decision. I could just be an okay actor or I could start to work out who I was and maybe become a great actor, and more importantly be a far happier person. I knew in some way it was going to require digging into how I had become who I was, but also reckoning with whether or not I wanted to be this person. Continuing in drama school brought this re-examination to the forefront. It was gift that changed me. I quite often forget that not everyone has this experience! Most of us are more likely to finish university and then get a job, whereas I had intensive therapy thanks to the demands of the theatre.

It was there in the church basement in South West London that Orange appeared. Orange decided on Orange's name … yes, I'm aware of the fruit theme in my life. As far as I'm aware, I am the only person to do a TEDx talk dressed as any kind of fruit. This had such an influence on me that I ended up having my 40th birthday party with the theme of everyone dressing up as their favourite fruit. It was brilliant fun! It all stemmed from the fruit salad metaphor in many ways.

Orange introduced Orange to me by a letter.

This is where I appeared! Whoop! Whoop! In my first letter to Em I wrote: (she kept it so I did not have to remember these words as remembering things is hard ... have you ever tried to remember loads of words ... holey moley its hard ... learning lines is BORING ... this is what I wrote..

Dear my best friend Em

Im so happy to be writing to you. Ive always been here – cheering you on, when youve been playing and open hearted that has been me willing you to see your light. I have seen sometimes how unkind you are to you and that makes me so sad that I feel smaller and I fade away a little, but I have always been here in your heart. Willing you to see the light that is you.

Together you and I can explore and have so many adventures. I cant wait. What I always see is theres so much colour and so much wonder that you sometimes dont see. Im here to help you stop and see it.

Please start to be as kind to yourself as you are to others.

Your very best friend.

Orange.

Yes that's my name by the way.

Like you, I've heard the suggestion that Clowns are products of trauma; a way that other parts of us show up. We all recognise the idea of an inner critic voice, don't we? I have yet to meet someone who does not have that "part" to them. Orange, Barbara, my podcast "guest star" and Frank, are not the same. Years ago, I wrote and researched a whole play on Multiple Personality Disorder. Having explored that world I can securely say that Clowns, and especially Orange, are not a sign of any unhealed mental anguish. In fact I would argue the opposite. Orange is the kindest part of me; the part that can see and feel kindness and witness the world through eyes of joy.

HELLO!– I'M ORANGE.

Its so good to meet you. You're truly a brilliant soul, I can feel it from here.

Oh, Im so excited that I get to be here with you. I mean properly excited. I mean Em is super on it and cool and everything, and she is letting me come out and play in this book. Its like her second coming out!! He he he he he he!!

I have always been around with Em and she has always known about me but it was brilliant to be able to write to her and tell her how awesome she is. I think she told you about the course she took when I was first allowed out to dance and play.

I have always seen Em has had quite a tough life, not only because of her childhood but how she took it all on herself. She has always had these awful thoughts of not being enough, def not loveable, and that she somehow doesn't deserve to be on this planet. That made me so sad to see. When I first properly emerged though I could tell her to be kind to herself and that all she had to do was allow herself to see things differently.

But enough of that and onto you – my darling darling you.

How wonderful it is to meet you and your lovely self – have you always been this lovely or have you just been getting more brilliant every day? When I look at you I see so much – your wonder and your curiosity is oozing out of you I cant wait to get to know you more. You and I are going to have so much fun.

So, there is Orange.

Now it is time for us to begin.

PART TWO

LESSON 1

BE SEEN

ORANGE'S OFFERS FOR YOU

Stop being scared of who you really are.

Stop and slow down.

Even though it's scary do it anyway –
you never know, you might like it.

Oh, yes you will. You can be happy!

FADE IN:

Large room, spotlight on solo mic stand in the middle – evening. EM STROUD enters wearing her favoured all black attire. The room is quite large, expectant and EM has a Britney Spears type microphone so she can jump straight into this – although for some reason they are playing Destiny's Child as she walks on. She dances for a moment. Smiles and starts.

EM

Can you see me? I know, I'm pretty short really! That is why I asked them to remove the lectern before I came on - so you could see me! In my show Re:Framed one of the threads is all about *Look at you* - yip that line of having the courage to really look at who we all are ... Yes, we do have to look at ourselves. And what I have learnt recently is that I am a tomboy lesbian (or some might call me soft butch) - I know right - I had no idea either that there are so many types of lesbian (seriously, there are loads, butch, femme, hard butch, alpha to name a few.) I used to hate that label. Less now though, so that's progress too!

So many of us are scared to look at who we are - but the weird thing is that the more that I do it, the easier it gets for me.

I mean I am now so okay with having clown sized feet - I know, right? Five foot two and size seven feet? What is she a gay pixie? Well yes, thank you. That is me! I could not have said that two years ago. Trust me. Being seen. What does that mean, you ask? Let's clear something up. I don't mean you have to start wearing a hi-vis jacket. (Disclaimer: If you move planes around for your work then definitely do carry on wearing one. In fact, if you're in any job where you need one … as you were). When I say be seen, I mean let's live as all of us. I'm not suggesting you stand in front of the mirror for hours staring at yourself trying to access some part of you that deeply accepts all your flaws. Imagine that scene! (Hey, if you can, then great - but really, will any of us ever reach that supposed nirvana? Me thinks not.) With a bit of work you can begin to see yourself fully. (I'm not a miracle worker - merely a Clown, here.) That's right, these words will only work when you do stuff. You can also choose to read this, laugh a bit, and then put the book down, or if you're up for being amazing, happy, achieving your own nirvana, then you'll practice all these lessons. I'm here to tell you that you could be feeling a whole lot different than you are now. That sounds delicious, right? [Aside: Like a good old fashioned jaffa cake - not, I hasten to add, the new variety to which they have added cherry into the mix. What's that about?]

The choice, my friend, is yours.

This being seen – you know what I mean, right? It's about allowing yourself to be all of you wherever it is that you find yourself. I know this is scary – you can't possibly let your boss see all of you, can you? You can't let your colleagues know your stories – like how you love playing sport, or that you are super into sci-fi and how you love all cats especially those called Monty. I mean that's just terrifying, isn't it? You can't possibly let everyone know that your relationship is at the breaking point because you have been working too hard. You can't show your team all your failures as well as your successes.

I wonder: Is that true?

Or have you constructed the idea of how you are in the world so carefully that you don't want to shift from it in case it changes how people feel about you? Do you resist the idea of altering how you show up to people because you think they may no longer like or respect you, or perhaps they might leave you?

I get it. And as we move post lockdown this being seen has never been more challenging as we have evolved, changed, and moved as people on the inside and the outside.

[Aside – I had a great chat about the reinvention of the outside of yourself with Lizzie Edwards on the podcast – all about style – if you do the inner work the outer work will change too! Listen in.]

Do you have that inner critic? If you don't, well done. You're the first human not to have one!

Do you always give yourself a really hard time? You know, like when you are in meetings and you tell yourself you're not speaking up enough, or you're talking too much and saying the wrong things? Or when you have to do that presentation and you break out in cold sweats for days in advance, and then after you do really well all you can concentrate on was how you had to refer to your notes to answer one of the dozens of questions asked.

Do you worry that you stumble over your words, or that you aren't as clear as you want to be? Do you spend time feeling anxious that you're not creating the impact that you want, or that you don't like yourself on video, or that you don't like your speaking voice … add your own self-deprecating inner chatter here.

I once worked with a man who appeared to have his life all sorted. He had a great family, and his kids were doing well. He had just been promoted to a new role. Yet inside his head everything was falling apart. When John stood up to deliver any of his messages at work, he thought he was doing so poorly. He felt certain the whole audience was judging him harshly. He had gotten to a point that he was trying to avoid doing any sort of talks, yet his team loved him, and audiences really enjoyed him. I wonder if you have similar challenges and are like John in some way …

I imagine you're really, really good at helping other people be brilliant.

And I bet you're super kind to everyone else.

So, why doesn't that kindness extend to you?

Ohhhh kindness I love that – it is sooooo important kindness…

Hey Orange, not yet, that's the next lesson, okay? We're still on being seen.

Whoop de whoop – okee dokee! Be you! Be cool!! Be seen – I wear braces they are very cool. I like them being seen, under my jacket.

That pesky inner voice is so good at ensuring you second guess yourself, and that voice is even more satisfied when you doubt if you can ever feel *really* like your truest self. If you could just let yourself be all of you then the world would be a lot easier to take, you know? There would be less fear of getting things wrong, and you would have the ease to move jobs if you wanted. You'd be more confident at sharing your ideas and participating in meetings. Life would just feel better.

How the hell do we get to that (realistic) state of just good old happiness? Well, luckily for you and me, we have Orange to look to for wisdom on this. Yes, it is going to take a while to fully let yourself be seen, just like it did for me. (I know … Shock! Horror! Not all these lessons just appeared when I was 21. If you're reading this and you're 21 then, Ta da! I've done all the hard work for you ☺.) Yes, here comes the part where you get to learn a bit more about me so I can prove that I do know what you're going through, and so you buy into me – I mean we are still early in our relationship right? (Rightly so, you are still sussing me out.)

I have always been visible. This is what twenty years of being a performer, speaker, and emcee will do for you! Even from the time I was at university, rather than taking a more traditional job I decided to be the DJ across town! Somehow, I have always found myself with a stage to be on and with a microphone in my hand. Yet, just as consistently I have been fearful of people *really* seeing who I was. (Here's a hint: it was all in my head.) But I didn't announce that I thought I was a chancer, or someone who really did not have a clue about what she was doing. Even more than that, I had this deeply rooted fear that I was just, well, fundamentally a bit shit, and that as a human I was not worth that much. As I mentioned earlier, I always wanted to hide my real self.

My "imposter syndrome" never showed up fully until I began writing the book you're holding in your hands. (I know the irony is not lost on me.) Orange had shared with me that being seen is a good thing, and that not being scared is a *really* good thing. Just because I'm the one writing the book does not mean that I remember all the lessons all the time. After all, we Clowns are human!!

I knew I wanted to write a book and start this new chapter of my life (see what I did there?) with some sense of permanence. The brilliant thing about the "roles" I have played throughout my life is that for all my being on stage and performing, etc., there had never been any trace of *me*, the *real me*, after I walked off the stage. I'd left (I liked to think) a good feeling, or some thoughts in people's minds, and often I had some sense of a job well done, but I never really left any slides in the traditional way and there certainly had never been a book where my words remained. This. This very act of being seen, here in these pages, is terrifying to me. As I write this, I am breaking all my rules. I know that I am not alone in having these rules. We all have them. The rules that only I know and no one else would imagine that I have, but that are as clear for me as starting my day with a cup a tea. (I mean, I'm British after all!!)

The fear of being seen can be attached to many things, many deeply held beliefs about who we are, what we can do and where we see ourselves in the world. The work I've done with my clients has shown me that fear of being seen is based on any of these concerns:

Fear of failure – *If I try something new, or if I change, then of course it will be a huge failure. It won't work, so why try.* We all know this one, don't we?

Fear of success – *I'm comfortable where I'm at.* We are so comfortable where we're at that the idea of succeeding is scarier than the fear of both failure and staying the same.

Fear of being "too out there" – *I don't want to be too much for people.* I know this one so well. It can feel too intimidating to be fully us and we worry about judgement, yes from others, but mainly from ourselves. When I launched my podcast Clowning Around I was worried that the idea of me being a Clown would be "too much" for people. I didn't think people would get it. Turns out they do get it and they like it. So, you gotta love the inaccuracy of our internal monologue, right? When have you made assumptions and they turned out wrong? Are you doing that right now?

Fear of not being "out there" enough – *I don't have anything significant to share.* Converse to the fear above, when I am working with people and they're telling their stories, those that have had a "normal" life always worry that their past isn't "out there" enough to warrant telling their story. They're afraid that no one will care about their experiences and history. This is just not true. Each of us has a story. You have had moments in your life that make you uniquely you. That uniqueness could help someone else change their life.

Fear of always being a failure in your own mind – *I'll just ended up screwing it up.* If you come from a background that was tricky like mine was, sadly we can be left with the feeling we will never be enough. In its simplest terms that is the legacy of trauma. If that is your truth, get professional help, I have had therapy for years now and without that support there is no way you would be reading this.

I wonder: Which of the fears above feels like yours?

Maybe this is a good time to get a notebook out. It's that time for you to do some thinking, (whoop de whoop) and start to write down what it is that stops you from being seen, from being fully you in the world in front of everyone.

What are your behaviours like at home versus work?

Do you ever wish that your work colleagues knew you have a brilliant sense of humour or that your partner realised you have a very serious side (or the other way round?) Do you wish that your parents knew who you are now so that you didn't have to revert back to being your teenaged self for them?

I have some ideas on how you can get over your fear and move past whatever is holding you back. I bet you're saying, *"Phew, thank goodness for that, or this book could be a crushing disappointment!"*

First, you must know deeply what is holding you back from being all of you. This is the start of not being scared by your own brilliance anymore. If as you read brilliance you baulked, because you don't think that you are brilliant … trust me, you are. We all are. It does not mean we all have to be famous, have huge social media followings, or in fact do anything other than allow ourselves to be all of ourselves. Knowing that you deserve to be you and be brilliant in all of you, that's your work.

We live in a world where the desire to be seen, to be visible, to be out there, is all consuming. Through social media, the pressure for how we are seen has only grown and will continue to unless we realise that as individuals, we have a choice, and we can be seen on our terms. We can take charge of who we really are. By allowing ourselves to be seen fully when we are happy with who we are, causes the fear to go. We mask up for approval when the pressure to be who we think we should be is ruling our freedom to be fully us.

We are so quick to judge and compare. The most damaging thing is that we do it to ourselves in the harshest and cruellest ways.

It is always easier to look at others than to look at ourselves.

FADE IN:

A large stage with full lights, and a lectern mid stage that will inevitably be sizeable enough to render not-very-tall performers invisible. EM STROUD enters wearing all black (what a surprise), a red silk tie, and silver trainers.

EM

Right, you lovely lot. Here I am. Yes, I'm your host for the rest of the event. I know what you're thinking, don't worry I won't be flirting too much with any of you fellas – have you guessed it? Yes of course you have, Sandi Toksvig and Sue Perkins (two famous lesbian comics and performers in the UK) were not available so you have me, the less well-known lesbian. Phew, now we have that out of the way shall we introduce our first speaker.

When I do the intro like the one above it's because I know what people are seeing. Me. A short tomboyish looking woman – who does look gay (shocking - as I am gay!!) So, I call them out on it. This is my tactic to make them feel safe. I'm joking about me, so that they can feel safe that I know what I am about. This is me verifying them seeing me. Which helps me see them and allows us to start to build a relationship as host and audience. When I do this, I actually watch them physically relax. They know that I'm okay and that I am open for humour and laughter. I used to do this as a default setting. It was only as I discovered and worked with Orange that I realised that by owning all of who I am like my height and my sexuality, and all the other external things about me, that I could be at peace with them. These words that used to feel like an attack by me on me no longer bother me. Working on my voice and who I am internally changed how I am showing up in the world for the better. I know that if you are reading this – that outcome would be good for you. [Aside: Carry on, MacDuff. Just a quick little Shakespeare reference there for you. You're welcome.]

I have worked with thousands of people to help them determine how they want to show up in the world – identifying the fruit or fruits from their bowl with them, and then allowing them the space to consider what they want their fruit bowl to be comprised of. When people are aware of their different fruit choices, the rest of the world and their opinions matter less. My one-on-one coaching clients continue to show me that by spending the time working on what is fundamentally them and what makes their hearts sing allows them to care far less about what others say.

Now this would not be a book with merit in the field of personal development, memoir, or the unique mix of other things I have in here if I did not mention Brene Brown at least once. Like many others, I love her work and if you have not heard of her – go seek her out. Her TED talk about vulnerability is brilliant. In one of my favourites of her books, *Braving the Wilderness,* she writes: "For me, if you're not in the arena also getting your ass kicked, I'm not interested in your feedback."

This feels true for me on many levels. When we truly own all of our fruit – (be that one or ten) – then we are active in our choice of how we want to show up, which makes being in the arena a joy, a calling. This is not me saying that you need to seek out fame or fortune or be some sort of superstar. You can be in your arena right now as all of you – be that a banana, a lemon, or any other type of fruit. I just want you to have the courage to really look at yourself and be brave enough to then let yourself be seen with all the beautiful blemishes and imperfections.

What I mean here is much more powerful and important than worrying about what others are saying about us. This is ultimately about knowing ourselves and tapping into how we are feeling. We need to pay more attention to that before we get into the realm of asking others. I know that we all seek out what our boss or our friends think of us, however those people have their own biases.

Could you change how much importance you place on other people's opinions?

A client of mine called Claire, who is a coach and speaker, once told me that she based her sense of how successful she was on comments left about her on feedback forms. Most comments would be good, however, she predictably focused on the one or two that were not so positive. In our time working together we changed her approach so she could focus on the good as much as the areas for improvement, realising that everyone has different filters. Instead of Claire going straight to other people's comments to validate how she had shown up in a session, she would immediately evaluate how she felt she had done. In essence, before she started to seek out other people's thoughts about her – she sought out her own thoughts about herself. We are the only ones that know what we are trying to do – so it's good to use ourselves in assessment.

Feedback is useful and important, however before we get to the point where we accept outside commentary as the fact of our performance, we need to be clear and awake enough to ourselves that we can see how we have done based upon our own understanding. We need to see ourselves in the mirror first before we let others into the view. I know this can feel scary – but the rewards are huge and will allow you a freedom that can make you unstoppable.

IN ORDER TO BE SEEN WE HAVE TO BE BRAVE ENOUGH TO LOOK.

I have faced my own fears, so I am not writing about something just in theory here.

In 2015 I wrote and created my first solo show called Coming Out of My Box and it had a sold out run off the West End of London. I was so anxious about the show, as this was me reclaiming the performing side of myself – and doing so in an autobiographical theatre comedy show. Up until that point I had never had the courage to share parts of my life. But I knew when I created the show, I would find answers or peace, or both. It wasn't me acting as someone else. I was not an actor nor a character. In completing the show, I recomposed parts of myself, pulling them from the boxes I had stored them away in.

The boxes were as follows:

Teenage boy, (except I'm a girl)

Businesswoman, (except I am a performer)

Victim, (except I'm not one)

Clown, (except I'm the observer)

Lesbian, (except I prefer gay)

Mother, no exceptions

Sex machine, (except I'm gay)

These were all part of me being seen again. I had been so caught up in the business world that I had stopped performing. The solo show was the beginning of me allowing myself to unite all of the parts of me again. I had a feeling that the joy of seeing all of me in the mirror would spark an interest in doing this type of work again.

You know the feeling. When you've been putting something off or ignoring a voice that says *I'm not happy*. As soon as you acknowledge it or see yourself doing something about that voice's remarks, deep in your heart you know that your life will change. It may not be immediate, but the seed of change has been planted.

In 2018 when I decided to write my second solo show, my collaborator Maheen and I considered content around identity. Often when I am working with people who are super smart and wanting to find more success in their worlds, we end up exploring not their mindset but their skillset and peeling the onion of who they are and what they want out of their life. This has been the same journey for me – getting to the place where I realise that I do not want to be boxed into a certain type of identity. I am the whole fruit salad.

In an episode of the Clowning Around podcast I spoke to Padideh Tosti, PhD about business consciousness. We talked about how the only way to shift the world in business is to awaken and look at who we truly are, to explore identity, and do what Orange says: Slow down. We have to be brave and ask ourselves questions about how we are showing up. I was reminded not just of the value of asking ourselves questions but just as importantly of having others ask us great questions.

In my professional life I have enjoyed looking at identity ever since I first discovered Robert Dilt's *Logical Levels*, a coaching tool to gain insight into where someone is struggling. I love the simplicity of his model – it helps anyone find exactly where their pain point, or most significant psychological challenge is. I have adapted the Dilt model over time. I start conversations, picking up on the cues that my clients say, to help me work out where they need support. When I first start working with a client, I always have this tool in the back of my mind. As a person moves up the levels, the challenges change, revealing how someone sees themselves. The Dilt model levels look like this:

Spirituality

Identity

Beliefs

Capability or competence

Behaviours and actions

Environment

Being seen is all about how we own our own sense of identity. In Dilt's model, Identity and Spirituality are high. Of course they are, it takes a lot more courage to look at who we are, to actually be all of ourselves, than it does to realise that where we are living is a bit shit and we want to move (the environment part of the scale). (It's a simple example, I know, but you get the idea.) Quite often when you take time to stop and look what is making you sad, it is the actual environment we are in. One of my clients who had been brought up in a city, moved out to the countryside as she thought that would be the next stage of her life. In her first session with me, she was feeling sad and unmotivated in every area of her life, and it soon transpired as we spoke that the countryside was making her feel flat, and that it has not fuelling her. It took some time and within a year she had moved back to the city and from that moment of realisation she felt better, and everything lifted for her.

[Aside – I promise, not everyone I work with ends of moving house and location. This was right for her.]

For me to show up in the world as the mum, friend, and human that I want to be I have to be brave and step up and look at these two highest levels in my life. Up until the last few years I was so fixated with my own self-critical beliefs, I doubted that I had the courage to step into being all of me. When I performed Coming Out of My Box I didn't know that this journey would lead me to writing this book, but it was the start of me shifting. Until that, I had not had the courage to really look at me and allow myself to be seen. I was still avoiding the mirrors both metaphorical and real.

Recently, I was interviewed on The Nicole Bremner Podcast. Nicole and I have known each other for years, it was only in this interview that I voiced my challenges of looking at myself in mirrors. Like so many women and more and more men, I have struggled with how I look, but before I could even dream of addressing that challenge, I had to look beyond my reflection and get to know who I am and who I want to be. As I have learnt – addictions, body perception challenges and so much more show up as a cruel way to avoid dealing with what is going on much deeper down.

FADE IN:

EM STROUD returns to stage.

EM

Don’t worry kids – it gets better. There is a happy ending here, I mean after all, you’re reading this book, so here is hoping she has some of the answers for us all hey … I mean who knew that in Lessons from a Clown there would be so much intensity – I thought she was meant to be funny.

(awkward silence)

HOW WE SHOW UP ... WHO WE NEED TO BE ...

We've lost our own notion of common sense and some would argue of empathy towards ourselves and each other as well. We have somehow set ourselves up that we must "be" a certain way, act or behave in a given manner that is socially acceptable and hide the rest of ourselves as people. You can choose right now to change that – allow you to be all of you. It is really liberating. Now you may well be thinking, "Sure that's easy for you to say Em, you're a Clown – you're one of those "out there" people. But I'm no different than you, it's just that I made the choice to really look at my life, at all that I am, and spent some time appreciating what I like about me. Then I got comfortable with that. What most other people think really does matter far less to me now. (I will always care about what key people think of me – that distinction is super important – another thing I learnt from Brene!)

So how do we do this? How do you get to a point where you can let people see the parts of you that you hide, like your silly side, your vulnerabilities, and everything in between? I'm talking about being silly if you are naturally silly, being serious if you are naturally serious, and just allowing you to be the you that you truly are, not the you that you think you should be.

GET OUT OF YOUR HEAD AND INTO YOUR BODY.

Let me tell you how this happened for me in two words: Clown dancing. The moment I fully understood for myself what getting into one's body can do, was when we were asked to do some Clown dancing. This was on the first of the two courses I did with De Castro – in the hall in Kennington, London. There we were on day three of my Clowning course and she brought us into a warmup session. Although I had always known that getting out of my head and into my body was powerful, it took me being Orange to see the impact fully.

Clown dancing.

I know.

I hear you.

A ridiculous idea, right?

There I was as Orange and I was dancing. As Em, I had a massive block around dancing. I was shite at dancing! Terrible! Two left feet that were oversized and attached to the short body with no sense of timing. I'd always had it. From the first moment in drama school, I'd felt like I couldn't really dance. Perhaps to be fairer to myself I should say that I hadn't ever learnt how to dance, and it seemed I was surrounded by people that had danced both here and at drama school since they were conceived.

FADE IN:

EM STROUD enters a small comedy club where the audience is seated in the round. She wears her black attire with bright yellow trainers. (They weirdly work well on her as they match her bright blonde bleached hair.)

EM

I mean, there I am, a short little frog – (I am not an actual frog, it was just how I felt, you get that, right?) I was in the corner, and I'd witnessed my friends and peers float across the room, nailing their pirouettes. They look elegant and genteel. (They're all in leotards and tights. Me? I'm in a baggy pair of trousers and poorly fitting tee shirt.) Then there is me. I look. I move my arm to where it is meant to be. I spin. And spin and then spin some more. Before I know it, I am not on the opposite side of the room and the corner as planned– I am in the middle of the room, spinning randomly, wondering when this torture will end. (Oh, that's right, it won't.) Now, I was learning a number from bloody Chorus Line. I was so useless, the only girl in the entire college that got dropped from that routine. Surely it would be over soon. Oh no … I was taught by an ex-Broadway captain (the best dancer on a show). He looked at me attempting another long forgotten dance term, and said, 'Oh

Emma, there really isn't much hope for you, is there?' I was in the front row. (Damn me for being small.) And I turned with confidence … until I was facing everyone else, not having turned, and there was me turning again to be the only one out of 60 people facing the audience ...

Nope, no idea where my block around dancing came from ... no clue ...

I am guessing this is similar to how many people feel about public speaking, giving interviews, or anything else that makes one break out in a cold sweat. That's me with dancing. So, there I was in my head at the De Castro course:

This is the most ridiculous thing.

I can't dance.

I look stupid.

I hate this.

Get me out of this.

Then Orange took over.

I have never heard this song! It is so exciting. Wow, look how my leg moves. Look how my hands move. I am amazing. Look at all these other beautiful people dancing with me. I LOVE it ... play more music please! I am free!

The music stopped and I returned to Em.

A shift happened with me was when I was in a therapy session, and it was being explained to me that my feelings are not me – they are only feelings. Huh? I thought what the actual ... but as we discussed it more, I started to get it. When I perform, I always get nervous, but I know and I like those nerves. They make me feel alive. They are not me. They are a sign to me. I recognise that for others nervousness can feel crippling. Our experiences of feelings can be different depending on how we interpret them. I just use nervousness here as an example, but it could have been anything. You know there are times when you are crying, and you think it will never change and you will always be crying. But it changes right, and those tears are not you, they are just feelings.

This is deep stuff!

On my podcast recently I explored this with Gordana Biernot when we spoke about all things My Power Talk. She is one of Oprah's Super Soul 100 teachers (so I reckon she knows her stuff!) She confirmed with me the importance of understanding that no matter how much we believe that emotions or feelings are us – they are not. They are only moments of life, and not who we are. They only become more if we give them power, or if we start to believe they are true.

I realised that in the moment when I was Orange, that my thoughts and my inner voice as Em could well be wrong and Orange's way of being could also right. At the start of the dancing exercise, I was getting in my own way. (Ever been there?!) I was still believing that dancing was something I could get wrong. I thought that while I was dancing, I looked all the ways I didn't want people to see me: I have no talent, I am out of rhythm, I am not a dancer, I am too short, I am too awkward to dance.

I was about to be reminded that none of those thoughts have any power if they aren't true. They only exist in my head.

Orange took me away from all of that and allowed me just to enjoy the dance, in my body. Who knew that was even possible? (And I was sober!!) Orange allowed me to just be me, and to allow others to see me dancing, and for me to have that freedom.

I wonder: What could your life be like if you allowed yourself freedom from your inner critic?

When was the last time you really felt free?

Have you hidden yourself?

Are you behaving as you think you should rather than as the person you actually are?

This experience led me to think about how we assess everything that is going on in our heads and bodies and life in general. Let's go back to the example of nerves. Nerves can be a super good thing, it just depends on how we use them and how we interpret them. There are butterflies, that anxiety we feel before something happens. (I am sure we all know how they feel right?) There are the nerves before a date you have been looking forward to. (You know the fab second date where you think you really might have found the one?) If you've been married a long time, just try to remember that feeling! For me, it's more recent as I was single up until this year – I know, lockdown love. Who knew it could happen? But it did! (Yip, she fell for the Clown line!) Because of years of mixed messaging most people believe that nerves are a negative thing. We associate them with times where things go wrong. Our brains are funny like that – we remember too well the things that we are not so good at, and the times that we failed at something. I believe we are taught that. Not enough attention is paid to the things we do well. We spend so long being told that we must work on our weaknesses.

Maybe we should spend time playing and working with our strengths? That could be a game changer for us all. Nerves are merely there to act as a guide. To show you that you're excited to be seen, and to be brilliant. You just have to know how to harness your power to ensure the response is excitement rather than fear.

When people are truly nervous, especially in times of stress or pressure, they often say 'It's my nerves' or 'Oh, I could never do what you do, I get too nervous.' I get it! I still get nervous – but I welcome that feeling. The day I stop getting nervous before a talk, a show, or a recording of my podcast is the day that I'll stop doing it. In my mind that means I have slipped into not really caring.

One of the techniques I use with my nervousness is grounding. In order to be seen by yourself, you have to allow yourself to slow down. Breathe and get yourself fully there in that moment. Feel the feelings.

Time, by its very nature is a human construct – yet we tell ourselves we don't have time to allow space, to breathe, or to slow down. But of course, we do. Unless you allow yourself the time to get off all the various treadmills you have created, how do you know where you're at? Of course, we all have treadmills we create and at the start they can be fun. Then after a while before we know it, we are just running from one to the next and just keeping up with living.

- Stop.
- Take a moment now and breathe. Deep into your tummy.
- Put your hand on your tummy.
- Close your eyes.
- Have your feet on the ground and breathe deeply.

There are countless books on breathing and its merits. If you want to explore more of the science about why it works go read one of those. The above practice is all you need to do. Daily. Consciously. This is the start of being seen.

Take a moment, check in with your treadmills and catch yourself moving from one to the other without pausing or stopping from parent to partner to friend to worker to gardener … (you get the idea.)

Do they still work for you?

Are they at the right speed?

Or as you stop do you notice that there are more rooms that you could go explore if you just walked away from a couple of the treadmills? When you allow yourself to breathe, I wonder if you'll see that there are other places and ways of life that are available to you. How good might that feel? I know, it's scary, but also just a little bit possible.

To be seen there must be a conscious decision that you are going to allow yourself to stop, slow down, witness yourself, and then allow yourself to hear you – all of you.

First, witness yourself.

When you do make the decision to ask the questions of life, to truly live and not just exist, and be open to being all of you, it is like jumping out of a plane with a parachute: you know the rewards will be brilliant and the journey will be magical but taking that first step (apologies for this example if you are reading this and have a fear of flying … change it into your head as you are jumping into the sea … or if you're scared of water just change it again into going on a journey in a new car – Phew! I hope I covered all the phobias there!) is tough.

I did my equivalent of the jump from a plane while on my Clowning course. (I was not expecting to.) In one exercise we stood in front of all our peers and just looked at them, and then took a moment to hold eye contact with each person – a conversation just through the eyes. I had to come from backstage, walk into the middle of the stage, and have twenty people see me. Me, Em.

I did not want to do this. I was so scared. This was in essence my worst nightmare – this was vulnerability at 100 percent for me. I knew that if De Castro thought we were putting on "an act" or trying to "do" anything she would send us back. I had to look at everyone. Silence. And then wait for my audience to tell me what they saw and how they felt.

Terrifying. My heart was in my mouth as I waited backstage. I had managed to go last because I didn't want to do this. I thought people would see how flawed I really believed I was. I thought they would see all the damage that I felt on the inside. I thought that they would see all of that and nothing else … my inner voice was winning. My own voice of fear.

I stepped out into the centre of the stage. I breathed more deeply than I ever have before, and I looked. I had eye conversations with people – with no words there was still so much said. These people, these fellow Clowns (many who are now firm friends) and I exchanged a dialogue of a kind. It was a shared profound experience. I took my time, engaging with everyone and after a few people I slowed down, enjoying this process and its tender nature. There was no need to speed through connecting with people, there was no need to be afraid. As I did this some of my audience cried, I was not sure why but instead of evoking fear in me, I felt as though they had let me into their hearts and their minds too.

I stopped as I got to the end of the line, making eye contact with each person. They were about ten metres away from me. I felt truly connected and also tired. Then I waited, I waited for their feedback through words of what they saw of me. My inner voice started to be cruel, bringing up different words than what I felt. I took another deep breath. Then I heard them.

They saw me. They saw me. They saw me.

Kind.

Vulnerable.

Open.

Someone with so much love.

Safety.

With a genuine little cheeky soul.

A lightness.

This was how I had made them feel. These words burnt through my beliefs about myself. These words were the truth of me. I had allowed myself to be unmasked and they did not observe that I was flawed, broken, or unlovable. I was more than okay. I was me.

That day on the stage at Clown school was the first time in my adult life that I had felt fully vulnerable and open. It was exhilarating, exhausting, and I was exuberant. I was Em. A human just starting, really starting, to own all of who I was and just possibly seeing how I could help others too.

To be seen:

- is a journey towards being kinder to yourself
- is allowing yourself to be fully in the moment

- is allowing yourself to write stuff down
- is allowing yourself to unmask – to let down the "should be" or "I think they like me when I am like this," and be truly seen and shine your light.

I love Julia Cameron's morning pages which she describes as one of the tools in her book, *The Artist's Way*. Every morning before you look at other people's worlds, get a cup of tea or coffee and a notebook and write three pages. These pages are not to be read back or worried over. This is a practice in hearing yourself. I have done this practice for years and it allows thoughts, concerns, dreams, and nonsense to all flow out of me without judgement.

After the eye contact exercise in my course that day something in me shifted – a door of possibilities had opened and so it's not surprising that the following day Orange appeared. Orange started to show me more about being human than I ever knew was possible.

LESSON 2

BE KIND

ORANGE'S OFFERS FOR YOU

Kindness has to be at the heart of how you live.

Kindness is strength.

Choose how you want to be in the world.

FADE IN:

On a small stage there is a single spotlight. The audience is in the round and the spotlight follows the speaker. EM STROUD enters wearing all black, with a silver tie and silver trainers.

EM

Ah yes, that kindness thing … of course, so simple, isn't it? I know, you're always so kind to yourself. There is never any whipping of self going on at all, is there? (I mean if there is, it's in the privacy of your bedroom, and that's fine, isn't it? Whatever gets you going is fine by me – no judgement.) No! You are *not* always so kind to yourself. When you do eventually allow yourself to really hear your inner voice, is it always cheering you on – 'You are brilliant!', 'You were so good at that presentation', 'In that chat with your friend who has really been pissing you off you were brilliant at putting in your boundaries and standing up for yourself!' Sounds like you, right? Thank God your inner voices are always so full of praise. I mean mine just love me! NOT! Imagine if the inner voices actually were kind … Imagine! Nah! It's too hard and too unlikely that they actually could be nice. Afterall, you have lived with your cunning self put-downs for years. Why change now?! It's just the way you are right? Or is it? Turns out there are things that you can do ... who knew...

EM walks off stage for the interval, there is a ripple of applause and a murmur of conversation starting up.

Talk to yourself nicely and with oodles of love, as it's nice to do that.

Never stop trying new things and things you thought you did not like as you probably do like them really if you let yourself. Go on, you know you want to. (Apart from truffle oil, don't try that again it's horrid.)

In the COVID-19 world one thing most of us have experienced is more time in front of the computer. We go to countless video meetings for work and for fun, caught in the trap of staring at technology on a frequent basis. I think this had added to how unkind we can be to ourselves in relation to how we are working.

I have been doing a whole load of gigs in the last year and one of the common messages I hear is how everyone has fatigue, especially fatigue from all these Zoom meetings. [Aside: Other platforms are available, Zoom has just been my go to.]

We have designed ourselves into a cruel, unrelenting pattern of expecting ourselves to be "on" all the time. People are working longer hours and taking less and less time for themselves. This is so unkind to our hearts, or spirits and just our human selves. Orange has taught me to really be in touch with my humanness – the connection and the way I talk to myself is so important.

I wonder: Have you been allowing yourself to be kind in your self-talk?

What would happen if you allowed yourself to take a full lunch break away from all screens?

I wonder: What would that feel like for you? I mean maybe just a cheeky little 20 minutes, and not even an hour.

At an online speaking gig a few months ago I asked this very question: How many of you are taking a lunch break? Only 10 of the 300 people in attendance were taking a lunch break. I found this to be so sad. This is just one simple act of kindness that we can do for ourself and we do it so rarely. Now is the time for this change. These small acts of self-kindness are important.

Another simple act of kindness came from the great Martin Lindstrom. I had him on my podcast recently, and he was talking all about Common Sense. One of his tips was to have meetings that are 50 minutes long. So, there are ten minutes between meetings. I mean, that's genius, right? So simple. Yet so kind. This is the heart of shifting our own relationship with being kind to ourselves. Small practical behavioural changes will allow you to have more space – allow you more time to breathe and I believe this will have a positive effect on how you feel.

I was working with Evelyn who is in a middle management role of a pretty big firm. She was smart, funny, and wanting to progress on her career. We had a call and I thought that she just looked tired. I checked in on her and asked what was going on. She said she felt pulled in so many directions, moving from one thing to the next, one meeting after another and then as soon as that finished, she went out of her office and was dealing with the kids. I just asked her – how many breaks are you having. She literally looked at me as if I was crazy. (This is quite a common response to me, and I have learnt not to take it personally!) We talked through why she was not having breaks, how she believed there was just not enough time, and as she started to say this, I watched a smile spread across her face. 'When did it get like this Em? I mean, I'm in charge of me after all and yet I am running from one thing to the next.' It was at this moment I knew she was slowing herself down so she could see the pace that she had been working at was completely unsustainable. I asked Evelyn, 'From next week on could you just put actual time in your diary, so there are pockets of time for you … maybe just try it.' Two weeks later we had a follow up session. She looked different, calmer somehow, and I asked how it was going. Evelyn said – 'It's a game changer Em – just these three little pockets of ten minutes each every day gave me a chance to breathe, to stop and check in with me. I feel so much more in control and so much better for everyone else around me.' This was the kindest thing she could do for herself.

It's good to do kind things for ourselves.

Remember me dancing at the De Castro course? As I left the church that day after the silence exercise and receiving my feedback, I noticed my surroundings. I could really feel myself walking, it was as if all the walking meditations I had done suddenly made sense. I could see the vibrance of the colours around me. I could feel how I was breathing, and was aware of every step I was making on the uneven grey London pavement. It was more appealing to walk the few miles on the wintery yet clear day than to feel trapped with other people on the Underground. My shoulders had lifted somehow. I felt straighter. [Aside: Don't worry kids, I was still gay, it was not one of those awful places. I had just moved my shoulders back a bit!] It was as if being witnessed had allowed something in my body to open.

We all hold stuff in our body. It makes sense, right? Something good or bad happens to us and there will be a physical memory. I'd always had round shoulders, something that I was already aware of and somehow this exercise made me feel as if they had moved back in a way. (Now, of course it is quite possible that they did not move at all – I know! But it felt as if they had, so I am taking that!) Actually allowing myself to be fully in my body was an act of self-kindness. Like many people, I have had my struggles with my body and up until 2018 I always thought I needed to accept that was just how I would be. I knew no other way to be and yet there are other, kinder ways to live.

It took becoming a Clown for me to be kind to me, in order for me to be in my body.

TO BE IN MY BODY, I HAD TO CHOOSE HOW I WANTED TO LIVE MY LIFE.

To be kind I had to stop letting life run away with me. People often talk about balance. I don't believe that there is such a thing as life balance. Yet, I do believe in choice. We can choose how we want to live our lives. Orange showed me that I could choose to be kind and live my life fully, but only if I was willing to try.

RAINBOW DIARY

I realised that to be kind I needed to operate in a different way, so I created my Rainbow Diary. Although I created this around the time my son was born – only when Orange appeared and showed me that to choose how I wanted my actual life to be was an act of self-kindness did I see the difference that small choices can make.

What most people do with diaries, including me in the past, is add work things, where the kids are, meet ups, and appointments. This is good but it does not go far enough. Take a moment get a notebook and write down seven things that you would love to have in your life weekly.

Here are mine:

Em Business (speaking, coaching, workshops, MCing)	Blue
Creativity Business (writing, creating shows, podcast)	Dark Green
William (my son)	Purple
Friends and Family	Red
Fun and curiosity (time with partner, classes, theatre, joyful things)	Orange
Exercise	Bright green
Self-care (meditation, massage, therapy, nails, hair, box sets)	Yellow

Each item has a colour assigned to it. On a Sunday night or a Monday morning I look at my diary and I put things in. Exercise, check. Self-care, check. These are both absolute musts. There is something about the conscious act of putting these in the diary that makes them far more likely to happen. I co-parent, so on the nights I do not have William I am up for doing lots of stuff, (sometimes to my detriment,) so the kind thing is to insert a large block of yellow time marked "go home and watch box sets".

Of course, I'm a realist, sometimes I'm travelling or really in deep with a project, so I might not have time to see any friends or family. This system makes me aware of that though. If I have not seen any red for a couple of weeks, I can be kind to myself and make sure that I put a whole lot in at a later point.

Now, I hear you, there are always a whole load of reasons why you cannot do this. I've seen and heard most of them.

"I DON'T EVEN HAVE SEVEN THINGS."

The Rainbow Diary can quite often highlight that your life is a really focussed on one or two things – perhaps too much Blue – the kind thing here is to realise, "Wow, it's time for a reset."

If you are struggling to work out what your seven colours might be, consider this: Has your work that was once a passion become just work? I once asked a CEO that I work with, 'Why did you start the biz?' As he responded, he realised that his feelings around the work at his tech firm had changed. He told me that he loved coding when he started, but now his role was about leading the business and he had no time to work on the part that he loved. Result? He added coding as one of his colours in the Rainbow Diary.

One brilliant lady got really sad when she realised she did not have seven things, which highlighted for her that there was a lack of fullness in her life. I asked her what she had really enjoyed doing that she had let go of because she was too busy, etc. After some time, she came back with the quietist of voices, 'I used to love to play the guitar but music was not deemed sensible.' She added music as one of her colours and now has lessons and practice time every week.

"MY DIARY IS ALREADY FULL FOR THE NEXT FEW MONTHS."

For some, this is a truth. Cool! Acknowledge that to be the truth and look for when the diary is not full and then start adding the colours that you want back in your life where there is space. Part of being kind is about seeing what is really going on in your world and doing things at the right time, taking away pressure. At the start of each year, I block out times for holidays, friends, and large chunks of creative time (otherwise I would never write and perform any shows). That is the kind way for me to turn up to myself, but this has taken me years to get to the point.

"I DON'T HAVE TIME FOR FUN AND CURIOSITY."

I have been lucky enough to be interviewed on quite a few shows and on one in particular, Glenn really pushed back about this idea of forcing "fun" time. He didn't initially like the idea that a person must put fun into the diary. He and I both agreed that spontaneous evenings in the pub were always better than those that were planned. Yet I would argue that doesn't mean it isn't a good idea to set the intention to have recreational time in your life. As adults we hope that fun and good times will appear, yet if we don't make a conscious effort then we are to some extent just hoping that life will turn out that way. (In the Be Playful lesson there are loads of simple quick ideas of how you can do this.)

This is also a really good way to be conscious with kids if you have them. I worked with a client who was a single mum to a 16-year-old son, and she was really stressed about not having quality time with him. We worked out this idea. Once a month, the two of them would agree to a budget and a time. One month she would choose what they did and the following month he chose. They both agreed to be open, kind, and engage fully in what the other one had planned. This shifted their relationship, and my client now happily goes to basketball matches, and has been in sound studios and shot zombies (she was less keen on this one).

"I DON'T HAVE TIME … "

You do. You are the only one in charge of your life. Right now, your life might not have time – but start putting all these things in when your diary is clear.

"I WANT TO GO OFF AND HAVE GOLF /SPA /RUNNING DAYS …"

If you are in a relationship, this is an amazing thing to do together. I have heard so many stories of resentment about people going off and doing their own thing and the partner is left dealing with the kids, etc. Do this as a partnership. Own what you want to do as individuals and who knows, go crazy and put in some date night times, or even weekends away. I worked with an MD recently who did this with his wife – he came to a session beaming and said – 'Em this really worked – I got to go off cycling for two days this month, she then went off and did her own thing and we have a weekend away without the kids.'

Life is about making choices for yourself, and kindness has to be at the heart of your choices. If we really acknowledge what we want or what we have denied ourselves then it becomes clear how much your life can open up. If COVID-19 has taught us anything, it is the fragility of life. None of us will look back and say, 'Thank God we sent those extra ten emails.' We will look back at the things that fuel us, which are at the very heart of being human.

Connection.

Joy.

Love.

Togetherness

Kindness.

Memories.

I had to allow myself to dance again.

I let myself feel the music and light and joy and that made me wake up to kindness. Being kind to self is not an option, it must become a way of being. It is not always easy, yet the rewards are there for us to all feel and witness.

Throughout my working life I have found myself in many strange and wonderful situations, that generally involve people and crowds. For a while, as I've mentioned earlier, I worked as a DJ. Half the time I worked cool events with good music. The other half of my DJ time I did weddings and other ceremony-type events. Oh yes, I was one of those DJs, with all the classics from ABBA to Gloria Gaynor to Britney. When I started off learning the craft of DJing I instinctively knew that if I used kindness and humour, I would be successful at it.

At most British celebrations there are two things – drink and more drink. Post the drinking, we Brits will eventually allow ourselves the joy of dancing. Having been lucky enough to travel to various parts of the world I know what a British trait this is. I wonder often if this is because we Brits are so scared of being seen, that we only allow it when we are drunk. Or is it a legacy from our pub culture and the gin times of the post-war Britain?

In Devon in the 90s there weren't too many girls DJing. It was a cracking gig for someone at university. I got paid well and drove my equipment around in a van. When I would start to set up there were always the idiots who would look at me then say, 'Where is the DJ?' There would often come the point where a guy (it was always a man) would come up to me and try and get super friendly … BAD IDEA, as I had a microphone … which I would turn on and ask him what his name was. He would say 'Stephen'. I would then grab the mic and say, 'Is someone missing her Stephen? As he seems to be a little lost and I think he needs his wife or perhaps mum as he seems to think he is a DJ.' Stephen would then go bright red and disappear … I would say this always with

"failure" to enter the binge/purge cycle did start though was a twenty-year dysfunctional relationship with food and it is only since I learnt these lessons that my habits have started to change. I mean, I now make beetroot and orange soup with a garnish of feta cheese and drizzle of olive oil. Oh yes! This is huge for someone who once ate only cheese. [Aside: This is no exaggeration, my entire diet in my 20s consisted of cheese on bread, pasta and occasionally cheese salad.]

When I think of food, I realise how far I have come with that relationship. Rather than beating myself up in my old unkind ways, I now celebrate my changing palate – this is a slow process and that is okay. One of the legacies of only eating a limited range of food is that now new food sometimes gets the same response from me as a weaning baby. (Yip, that's right. I throw it across the room in disgust! Not really…)

Most of us have something that we beat ourselves up about – how we look, or what we are doing for work. We question whether we are in the right career, wrong business, right business, and why we are not doing what we want to do. We criticise ourselves for how much money we have or don't have, and bad business choices … the list is endless. I believe the inner voice is there to guide us. Even what we can think of our "worst" parts of us are just bits that we are not so comfortable with. (I explored this with my friend Hazel Gale on the podcast where we were "Clowning Around … Mind Monsters". Her book is really worth reading!

Dance was one of the things that I could speak unkindly to myself about.

Until it wasn't.

As Orange took over.

I LOVE dancing – when I was told we get to go to the Clown disco I was SOOOO excited I could not believe that it was possible to be as excited and as happy doing something. The music started and I got to move. It was to songs that I know Em had heard maybe 1000 times before. The first one was Dancing Queen – it was the first time I had heard it. The music got into all of me and before I knew it I was lost in the world of ABBA. I was there meeting my fellow friends – we were smiling and looking at each other and I felt so alive. When I dance it is as though I'm flying, it is SOOO exciting and brilliant. Sometimes I moved slowly. Other times fast. And with my big, brilliant jacket on. Sometimes I put my hands in my pockets, sometimes I didn't, it didnt matter.

See that girl / Watch that screen/ Living the dancing queen

Oh I could dance for ever. All I know is how it makes me feel like I think how a puppy would feel every time their owner walks back in. Oh, it is so good. So I danced and I danced and I danced until we did not dance anymore because we were going to play something else – I always know that I can always dance though which is a pretty cool feeling.

I have an unbelievably low tolerance for ABBA. This is what DJing at weddings will do for you. Yet there I was – well there Orange was, linking two of the things I thought I hated most, dancing and ABBA.

Ever since drama school I had linked dancing with achievement. My lack of skills, I had connected to the issues I had with my body and my challenges. There in that moment, as we stopped the Clown disco I realised something. I had just done dancing differently. I had felt kind towards me and my body.

Something had shifted.

In the weeks after completing the Clowning course I started to allow kindness into my life more and more. I learnt the simple act of asking myself, *What would a kind thing be to do?* This opened up so many options. I started to want to explore different things in every avenue of my life. I tried lots of new things, shifted my routine, started to live in a different, kinder way.

Don't get me wrong, I am not going to be going on Strictly anytime soon (and if I do, I will be more Ann Widdecombe than Aleshia Dixon). However, what this has meant is I am now willing to be kind to see what I can experience and how things will feel.

At a speaking gig recently, we were talking about how being kind was so important for maintaining our mental health. What struck me was that all the audience responses to kindness were automatically about other people. When I pushed a bit deeper, I felt and understood that there was a reticence about putting themselves at the top of the to-be-kind-to list. What I argued to them was – if we are not kind first to ourselves then how can we expect others to follow our lead (this was a gig for leaders of an organisation). They spent some time discussing kindness and how it was vital that they used it in their company.

I left them with something to ponder.

I wonder: What could being kind mean to you each day if you spent time consciously using kindness as a driving force of your behaviour?

What could that mean to you too?

As with Being Seen, Being Kind takes work. It is a conscious and consistent act that involves choice.

Use and create your own Rainbow Diary. Go and do what makes your heart sing.

Listen to what you would tell your best friend to do.

Be kind – get support, create a support team around you who are not just your friends – there are free and paid resources – use them.

Allow others into your head so that your inner voice which is often the source of a steady supply of unkind words, can be balanced out with kinder, gentler truths – this does mean being brave –

BEING KIND TO OURSELVES IS THE BIGGEST ACT OF BRAVERY.

I like to view it as allowing all of me – there is not one moment that I am not aware of what is around me and what I am holding and what is possible there are always so many possibilities if you just see them, that is why when you walk up stairs there are so many options of how you walk up stairs, it's amazing ... yet I notice that most people just walk up them ... how boring!

Ha ha, love it, Orange! Yes, the stair thing was yet another realisation I observed. We all do things on auto pilot. Of course, we have to in order to get on living, but what kindness does it take to allow ourselves to slow down and check in and see if we are doing things in the best way?

One of the kindest things I have ever done for myself was acknowledge that the way I was living wasn't the best it could be – I was not choosing how I wanted to live, I was being dictated to by myself and others, always on the reactive foot instead of the proactive one. I used to fight structure – I did not want to conform to times or ways of behaviour, it was not some anarchistic part of me, it was more about choice and not having to follow the rules that others were. Upon reflection I realised that in my resistance I was being unkind to myself and ultimately, I was missing out on things that would have made me happy.

This imbalance, this unattainable notion of a work/life balance is something that I see frequently with my coaching clients – we're all seeking it. Whatever it means to us. As I stated before I do not believe in balance – I believe in choice and choosing how we want to live. Yet, this is a place where I witness a lot of unkindnesses toward self. When we aren't choosing, we are responding, and reactive behaviour is less conscious behaviour.

Regardless of their situations, job level or if they own a business, people are always craving a shift in one way or another.

To create any shift in your life – from new job, to having more confidence, to finding a new partner, to divorcing your current one ☺, to creating a new business, you must start by being kind to you.

For some of you this might be the most difficult thing, if you have grown up in a world that has not been kind to you, it is easy to harden up and to believe that the hard you is the real you but it's not. It is a result of what happened to you. It is not you.

You. Yes, you reading this, are full of heart, full of love, full of possibilities, full of dreams and hope.

I wonder: Can you allow yourself to feel that; to close your eyes for a moment and breathe in all your goodness?

Right now is the time to be soft, kind, and gentle to yourself.

Who knows, you might even learn to love to dance.

LESSON 3

BE PRESENT

ORANGE'S OFFERS FOR YOU

Enjoy each moment of life.

Being in your body, not just your head.

Allow for wonder in the small things.

FADE IN:

EM STROUD enters wearing her typical all black attire and LEGO trainers. (*Yes, these trainers exist and yes, they are part of EM's vast collection. It's possible that she engaged in a bidding war on Ebay to get them.)* She is on a large stage and carries a roaming microphone.

EM

Ah, that being in the present thing – that old chestnut, hey? I mean you know it's a good idea, right? But really, who does it? Who actually stops thinking about the other 9000 things that you have on? And let's face it, that is why social media was invented, right? To take us out of the present and move us into that ever-so-important world. Social media is real, right? And that is actual life, isn't it? Not the one that you're living right now! Who here does not love a random scroll for, I don't know, an hour? It's funny, hey? We all say we have no time … yet we always have a bit of time for a good old social scroll. (When I say a bit of course I mean at least an hour.) Now, of course, not being present has always had its advantages. In that boring old meeting where John (sorry to the Johns reading this) is going on and on about something that you do not care about. But that same old meeting is the one where your boss is watching you and you are so clearly not present and then they ask you a question. Oh yes, we have all had those moments. That sinking feeling when all the world turns their attention on you and you have no idea if they were discussing windows or Winnebagos.

EM leaves the stage and the audience members start to get up and go get drinks from the bar.

Ahh to stay present, to allow myself to just do that one thing that is in front of me. While I was writing this very book there were so many things that could take me out of the present, so many distractions that were calling me.

Just look at social media.

Just quickly check that my emails have all sent.

Just let the dog out.

Even passing through the edits later, I was shifting over to just double check my emails. [Aside: I just did this RIGHT NOW. There were four emails screaming to be answered – I nearly responded and then I remembered I was supposed to be focused on editing the Be Present lesson.] So I turned my attention back to relearning my own lesson and the emails waited. Go me!! Or we could just rearrange that bookshelf for the fifth time as it must done right now, after all.

With this in mind, let me ask you this: If you allow yourself to be present, can procrastination fall away? Put simply, yes. Procrastination at its essence is about taking you away from the things that you know you should do or think you want to do. How many of us have found ourselves in a place where we know we should do our tax return but actually the kitchen really needs a thorough cleaning? The skills of being present will help you identify what is going on for you as you start to organise those DVDs that you did not even know you still had, rather than the task you actually want to be doing. (Yes, I do still have some DVDs – I can own that! They're classics.)

Being present is not only about achieving outcomes and avoiding the pitfalls of procrastination, but also mostly open space to be in where you can find that magical state of flow. Now come on, you know this. It's that place where everything you are doing is easeful. It's that place where regardless of what it is you do, you are allowing yourself to show up and be in that moment. It's that place where you have done all your preparation and you know what you are doing, and why you are there. It is the days that you look back on and say, today was a good day.

I was talking to Joanna Gilbert on my podcast about this very thing – we were "Clowning Around … Art". What struck me about how she produces such a great deal of brilliant work was that she isn't afraid to be fully present. She has a playlist that helps her "get in the zone" plus when she is in her studio that is what she is there to do. I found this when I was creating my last show. There is something about being in a physical space that signifies to my brain that I will be present to just the work I am wanting to create. I appreciate that both these examples are practical and creatives roles – the interesting challenge for me is allowing myself to enter the same space mentally if I am on a computer. What has worked for me is creating an environment within my "office world" such as having the playlist, and turning off notifications. [Aside: yes that's right, even your WhatsApp notifications … did you know you can turn them off just for an hour, or eight hours? Yes, it's okay if you do not respond to all messages as someone else sends them! Who knew! I do not have to reply about the cake sale the PTA is organising just because the president is messaging me right now!! Whoop whoop, permission granted!]

Being present requires energy. It requires attention, and therefore we sometimes choose not to enter this state. We are all fully present when we are at a job interview or in a high stakes situation, but I wonder why we don't choose to be in that state all of the time, because it does allow us to be at our best. Orange reminded me of this.

That brick on the wall. The light coming through the sky light – look at the clouds rolling by. They are wonderful. Look at how the floor has different lines in it. And if I walk on this step it squeaks. We just get to see. We just get to look in the room its so good we have three hours just exploring, have you any idea the true majesty of the church hall I am in?!!! There are so many things to look at and see its brilliant.

I noticed all these things as Orange when we were doing our "being in the room" exercise. I'd done this during my theatre training, but I'd never experienced being present like I did through Orange's eyes. This is an intense version of being present. I am not suggesting that you might start going around your house and staring at your floor. It grounded all the experiences that I'd had teaching others to be present in my business career. It took me deeper than the ruminations of an improviser.

A few days later in my favourite London coffee shop I got a taste of this change within me. The shop is just on a common in London. It has creaky wooden floors and loads of books and unusual items on the walls, oh, and the coffee is fantastic. There are a variety of places to sit – some for people on laptops, larger benches for groups and on that day there was one group that caught my eye. It was a mum, her son, and an adult friend. The boy was around 3-years-old. The adults chatted and ordered their coffee. The boy though, was not bothered about food or drink, he was looking around. He picked up the cushion on the seat – he looked under it, he looked under the table. He picked up a book from the shelf. All this looking came about while his mum was ordering coffee. She then turned her attention to him and told him to sit up on the chair like a big boy. Then it struck me. As adults (unless you are Clowning ☺) we've chosen to stop really seeing, to stop looking. We've stopped exploring the world with all of our senses. That is the fullness of being present. When I am Orange the fullness of each moment is as close to a spiritual experience as anything else I've had. Orange allows me to be so present that the one moment that concerns me is the one I'm living.

Right here.

Right now.

[Aside: Apologies if I just put that Fat Boy Slim song in your head … it's quite an ear worm, right?]

I get that we can't spend our time savouring each moment in extravagant detail or pay that level of attention to everything we touch or are involved in.

I wonder: Why we are so fearful of living more presently and attentively? Orange showed me that the present is what we have and enjoying the process is as important as any outcome.

I chatted through all of this regarding mindfulness and its relationship with Clowning on the podcast with Louise Chester who created Mindfulness at Work 15 years ago and has been taught by some of the great teachers. One of the key takeaways from the conversation is that mindfulness is coming home to yourself. Orange brought me back to me in so many ways

In the UK, from early childhood we are all about outcomes. We go to school from 4- or 5-years-old and pretty much have outcome-based expectations placed on us by the education system and other societal institutions from then on. This system is in part the reason that we are as adults are so fixated on achieving. Look at Finland, where the kids do not go to school until they are 7-years-old. Until then they are allowed to play. Play is enough. I will explore the Lesson of Play later in the book, but I think it is important to acknowledge that we are massively conditioned to seek outcomes at the cost of free action. For us to be happier humans this must be challenged, and we have to allow ourselves to change the way we operate.

In the conversation with Padideh Tosti I mentioned previously when we were "Clowning Around … Business Consciousness" I came to understand that for us to really excel at whatever we do – at anything from an Etsy shop to being a CEO and from being a civil servant to a shop worker – we must allow ourselves the space to question how we are showing up to the world of work. As an improviser, one of the main skills that I have developed is Being Present. There are two ways to access that state – the first is breathing. Ah yes … breathing. You remember the key choice we looked at in Lesson One? How is that going? I hope you are doing it now!! [Aside: Reader friend I know how difficult it is to implement this stuff. Don't worry, I've got loads more things coming your way to help you. Take a moment to pat yourself on the back. You're halfway through this and I keep banging on about breathing.]

I hear what you're thinking, 'We get it Em, alright? We even have watches that tell us to breathe.' I know you're all expecting me to tell you how this can be easy and the realisation that you have to do this yourself if hitting hard about now. 'Blimey, Em, and I thought this book would help me change me! Can't believe I actually have to do something in order for that to happen.'

I've got you. Change takes effort and you want change ... we all seek shifts, remember?

Read on.

TO BE PRESENT, YOU HAVE TO CONSCIOUSLY CHOOSE TO LET YOURSELF BREATHE.

This is how you can change how you show up and how you feel. You must consciously breathe into your tummy. Do it now. No, don't pretend to do it and move on.

Do it now. Just notice how you feel.

Do it again. Okay, you may now continue. Who knew a Clown could be so demanding!

The other part of being present is intent. Taking a moment to be conscious about how you want to show up will allow you to adjust your reaction to any situation.

Intent is about choice.

I was working with a sales director of a big firm, I'll call Steve. Steve was unsurprisingly good at selling their services. Yet he was finding that some meetings went better than others and he wanted to up his game, so he found me. Our conversation went like this:

E – So what do you do to get yourself ready?

S – Well I look at the agenda, or if I've set it, I look at the people I'm meeting and work out what I am going to say. Normally I look at the slide deck, refresh it a bit, and then go in.

E – Oh, okay but what do you do to get yourself ready?

S – Um … not sure I know what you mean.

E –What you're telling me is that you get the "what" you are delivering ready, but I am more interested in the "how" you are getting yourself ready.

S – Um, well, I make sure I look okay.

E – Well that's good – can I help you out here?

S – Yes, please.

E – So, what are you thinking about in terms of how you want to be seen by others? What's your focus?

S – Well, I want them to buy.

E – Of course you do. However, unless I'm mistaken you cannot get into their heads and actually influence that, can you?

S – Well, I guess.

E – So, who can you influence and be conscious about?

S – Well, me.

E – Exactly. So, for you to be most likely to get the outcome you want – what behaviours, or rather, what intent could you choose to show up with?

S – Like an emotion?

E – Yip, could be.

S – Well, I guess if I went in and was clear and concise and engaging that would potentially work.

E – Brilliant.

In this interaction Steve worked out that for him to potentially get the outcome that he wanted, which was the sale, he could choose to focus on himself. This is such a vital part of being present.

FOCUS ON WHAT YOU CAN CONTROL WITHIN YOU, NOT ON WHAT YOU THINK IS GOING ON AROUND YOU.

Easy to say, yet sometimes so tough to do. I know.

I was doing a gig to a room of 600 doctors, and I was feeling the nerves. Here was me, the Clown, the improviser, doing the keynote after watching professor this and professor that give very detailed (yet non-interactive) talks, which were surely of huge medical importance. They were not boring per se ... not saying that, just maybe a little boring to my fun-loving ears. My inner voice was having a field day.

You should not be here.

They will not get you.

This and you are going to be far too much for them.

They will not get it.

The Chair (that's right, no emcee at these gigs – just a very grown-up Chair) called my name and the ripple of applause summed up the energy in that room and what I read as the pure scepticism of me, the little pixie appearing on stage. I knew I had to focus on my intent. Focus on me and trust that my content and my delivery were what they wanted.

I took some deep breaths and I looked at the little mind map that I do for talks and reminded myself of my intent. I put three key words in a circle in the middle of the mind map and then the stories and content messages around this. For this gig the words were: educate, engage, fun. I had made a choice with educate as I expected this was most likely to hook their attention from the start.

Well, that was my hope, anyway.

So, I started in, my tone reflecting *educate*. I was calm. I had authority. I was in flow. I was present. Then as my talk continued, I shifted to engage and fun and I was getting them all standing up and trying stuff, and then

I *saw them*. Although over 580 people were up and doing what I asked, at one table right at the front the attendees were all sitting down, talking, and not looking as though they were with me at all. Of course, my very human mind chose to focus on them. (Like when you get reviewed at work with 95 stellar comments but obsess over the single bad one. Come on, I know you do that!!) I could not be fully present with the entire group then. I was taken out of the process of delivering the talk. I reverted to outcome focus and in this situation the outcome was getting this table engaged. I had to catch myself. I took some breaths, went back mentally and cleared my head and re-focussed: educate, engage, fun.

I continued.

I finished the talk (and I got far more than a ripple of applause), so I resolved that the outcome had been pretty good. But my head was still reserving room to question if I had gotten it right, whether I had shown up with the right intent, since that table wouldn't try anything. On a break, everyone from the disengaged table approached me en masse. 'Em,' one of them said, speaking for the group, 'We loved you. So sorry that we were talking and not doing, but we were trying to work out how we could get you to come and talk to our board.'

Lesson learnt.

First, don't do a mind read of your audience. It doesn't matter if that audience is one person or 1000 people. It is likely you'll be wrong. To be present means you must be present to you. I'm not saying don't acknowledge or be aware of your audience. Just don't give away your power. We base too much of how we are present upon what others say and think. Intent is a deeply personal choice. That choice will work best when it is linked with who you are AND who you are when you are at your best as well as when it is aligned with what is important to you, or what you value.

This is a list of intents that resonate with me as they are linked to everything that is important to me:

Fun Engage Curious Direct
Motivate Happy Listen Educate
Playful Calm Reflective

These are my words … other intents that others have used over the years include (this is not a complete list!!)

Inspire Thought-provoking
Confident Gentle Authority
Conscious Clarity

I wonder: What would your intents be?

What would work for you?

A brilliant client once decided that she would have a five-minute meeting with herself at the start of the day. She would look at the meetings she had in her diary, and what her intent was for each of the meetings. She reflected the following back to me:

'Em, I am so much more conscious about how I am showing up, rather than just turning up. I feel like I can contribute so much more as I feel really in it. Plus, taking a few breaths before I go in so I can be fully there is helping. It also has meant that I have not gone to so many meetings as I actually realise I have choice! Plus, the response that I am getting is so much better – it is as if by me being more involved has shifted others as well.'

This made my heart sing.

Allowing yourself to be present is the biggest gift to you and all the people you are with. But how do you know if it works? How do you know if being present has actually served you? In a word: reflect.

Ha, Ha. I love this so much! I love the moment. The look. The moment in time, that being. I am so happy when I am allowed to be immersed in the space I know that I am content in. When I had to do the being in the room exploration everything was possible. I got to spend an afternoon just in wonder of the space that I was in. I saw so much and I got to watch the clouds move – they kept changing, all the time. Every time I thought I had seen them all then they did something else. It was amazing. I wonder when you last looked up at the sky and just watched ... it is soo cool.

In theatre when we start work on a show, a director gives us notes. They are only there for a short period of time though, and then we are left to our own devices. So, after every show it is key to take some time to cast the gaze back and seeing how we've done. We ask ourselves what we could have done better, etc. The audience will, to an extent, have given us some acknowledgement but it is not there to help us get better. That is not the audience's job.

This is true of life, don't you think?

TO BE PRESENT WE MUST ALLOW OURSELVES TO REFLECT.

Only we can give ourselves the space and permission to change and to grow. If we start to change how are in the process of living, then we need to stop and reflect in a different way. To be present. To be fully living requires an energy, an act of choice and a bravery that is far more than existing.

The high state that Orange describes was just that. I literally felt as if I had taken drugs and was having some sort of spiritual revelation. (Probably because I think I did.) It became so clear that if I allowed myself to be fully in that moment I could see and feel so much more than I had been allowing. Like the kid in the coffee shop had shown me.

Life using these lessons changes us. It becomes brighter, louder, and also quieter, and it becomes more, well, alive.

Who doesn't want to feel that?

It's so easy to be caught up in the world of existing – I know. I believe I have done it for 38 years. I was so scared of being present to all of me, of allowing feelings, that I managed only to create a world that looked as though I was living it. I was playing it safe.

I view it as a simple scale.

If you take a simple intent – say, engage.

Look at this.

0 1 2 3 4 5 6 7 8 9 10

Engage

Where I'm going dictates where on my scale I will pitch my intent. What I mean is, if I am at a comedy gig my engage would be a 8 or 9. If I am at a bank doing a gig on storytelling I might go to a level 5 or 6. Of course, when I get there I assess and move up or down the scale as needed, but it gives me a position of strength to start knowing where I think I want to be on my scale.

Being Present in your own life is like this scale conceptually.

I used to exist living somewhere between a 4 and a 6 of my own scale of anything. I was too scared to feel all the feelings. Both positive and negative. I was afraid that if I allowed myself to go too far down in the numbers I would get stuck there and never come back out. I could never allow myself to go to the high numbers, either. So, I played safe. I noticed how much I had changed recently when I was featured on Dr Mandy Lehto's Enough podcast. After the interview I reflected on how I had moved around on my scale. I set my intention to be open and brave. I really was and after the recording I felt a deep sense of vulnerability and pride. Pride that I had allowed myself to be so fully present in the conversation and pride that I had allowed myself to be an 8 or 9 on the scale of my intent.

It's possible to live differently. I'm proof. It is the height of consciousness, choice, and yes, of personal leadership, and it is quite possibly the strategy that you get to experience the fullness of life. To Be Present I had to come to terms with looking in a mirror, and to see who I am with all my faults, insecurities, behaviours, and patterns. I had to allow myself to feel the emotions that I had boxed away. I had to allow myself to explore what it was that made me me.

> I remember when we were doing Em's last show there was this lady who came and sat at the front – she had this amazing necklace on and her eyes ... she had these eyes and that the necklace just showed me how kind she was – she was radiant, she was so full of living. So, I told her how beautiful she is. It made her cry (not in a bad way! I promise!)

Orange is so in the present. (Yes, one could argue akin to the boy in the coffee shop.) Orange can only say the truth and is so much braver than me in owning that truth. I would never have said that to a member of the audience, it would be too much of a personal interaction, even for me. However, what Orange allows me to do is to see the truth and to have the courage to say it. Orange is so present to life that there is never a moment where things can be not be said and truths not told or skies to be wondered at.

Yes, being me is fun!!

After being as Orange for the first time that it is possible to see the world in so many ways. So how do you do that if you are not a Clown, you ask?

I believe in writing. I believe in writing with a pen and paper. I have already mentioned Cameron's Morning Pages and their benefits. I would also suggest a process called feedforward which is rooted in appreciative enquiry and positive psychology. There are brilliant books on both but the simplest way of pulling it all together for our purposes are these questions that Deon Newbronner and I adapted.

What have you done well and should do more of?

What could you do to improve next time?

What are you grateful for in self?

I always suggest to clients to buy a new notebook (Whoopppeee!!) and use that as your feedforward book. Once a week put a ten-minute meeting with yourself in your diary and write down your answers to these questions. Perhaps you were just trying to breathe more in a meeting. Once a client came back to me with these answers to that new choice for her, she said:

"I was really good at breathing at the start of the meeting, and it made me feel calmer and less emotive with some of my team.

I will improve if I keep focussing on my breathing throughout the meeting, as halfway through I forgot, and as a result my pace of speaking sped up and I was not listening as well as I could have.

I am grateful that I am trying this new way of showing up as it is making me feel better."

She then said how much just the act of writing these questions down really helped her and took her out of her head for a few minutes and she could see how doing this regularly would be so useful for her.

I wonder: How could this help you in your life?

Would reflection (in writing) allow you the chance to see what you are doing well, and also highlight what you want to improve on?

Being Present means being conscious while living. It means experiencing life in your body as well as your head. Yes, we all find it easier to stay within the small scale of existing. It is safer. And, in many ways, it is what we are taught to do from early childhood.

Part of this Being Present is about not pushing to get there. If we push, we are forcing; we are only seeking outcome. We are putting the wrong energy in.

I'm reminded of the massive number of times I said to my therapist with, 'Am I really slow in getting this?' She always responded with, 'Getting to what? Pace is always in your mind anyway. It will take the time it takes.'

But seriously, can being present really help in life and work?

Yes.

People often ask how I create shows. Do I write it all? Then edit? Do I make it all up and speak it out loud? What do I do? With theatre and my type of shows it is all about (Yip, you guessed it) Being Present.

I often have moments where an idea or a theme pop into my head, or there is something I want to explore. My last show started from a conversation that stemmed from the work of Robert Dilts and considering my identity. I was fascinated by what people view as identity, and how we create identities around what we consider important. I started to collate information I collect during research about bravery, trust, discipline, curiosity and more. I then met up with my co-creator Maheen Mohammadally to explore what and how we thought this could work into a show.

We showed up to the process. We allow ourselves to Be Present to what we are wanting to create. We talked. We wrote things up on whiteboards and tried out various stories. We allowed themes to emerge and played with all of them. During this time of devising, we fully immersed ourselves in this world. When we had a break, we had an actual break – we didn't check emails. (It is so common when I work with people in business and I give them a break and they instantly get onto their devices. This is not going to help anyone. Once you get on a device you are no longer Being Present at the meeting. You're mentally darting in and out of different worlds and not fully inhabiting either. This is the challenge of modern day living.) Again, these Lessons from a Clown take effort and choice. To Be Present you must actively choose to be. As I write this book it is because of my Rainbow Diary that I have the space to Be Present to write. Otherwise, this book would not have happened!

To aid you with simple ways of getting more conscious in your time, so you can choose to Be Present I really suggest you read https://maketime.blog/ where you'll find loads of great tips that will help you Be Present of your life. If you are doubting the power of how Being Present can affect you, and you want a deeper and longer explanation of this then read Cal Newport's *Deep Work.*

So, as we are working on the show, my writing partner and I do not focus on any outcome. (Of course, we have an awareness that we have to produce a show by a date in the diary, that is the only important time milestone we have. To be present doesn't mean you won't have deadlines and goals. The show starts to appear. The themes start to become clearer.

For *Me:Em* the name appeared during one coffee break. It became really clear that in order to do a show up about identity I would have to explore my own.

Fuck.

That was not what I expected would emerge. I wasn't sure I wanted to talk about it. Yet Being Present allowed me and Maheen to see what needed to be told right now.

Of course, if you are reading this you could say, "Okay that's fair enough, Em. But that's the creative process. I get that from an artistic viewpoint there needs to be time and space for creative projects to develop. This however is not real life." You have kids, a husband, a wife, a mortgage, and a grown-up job – you don't have time for all of that taking space and reflecting. Life is too fast.

If you are having these thoughts and challenges, I so get it. I was once so caught up in constantly responding mode that I was not proactive in my life. I was reacting to my world. I was reacting to others.

When that happens to me, I go back to my Rainbow Diary.

If we do not proactively create time for ourselves, we cannot Be Present.

You can only exist and be reactive to others and not yourself. This is your choice.

Can you choose to put you into your world, so you do create time or is there always going to be a reason why you do not allow yourself the time that you deserve?

This is a shift; a change in behaviour at its deepest level. It is about showing up to you and your processes and what you want and not about waiting for the right time.

Speaking personally, about my show, there was never going to be a "right time" to write a show about my childhood, including the challenges that I had, the emotional neglect, the grief. I've got to be honest; I would happily never have written those stories down. But that would have been me allowing fear to guide my response. Not writing the show would have been me existing, not living, healing, or processing.

This is clearly my story, my choice of life and my calling to do these things. You don't need to write a one woman show about your life (though do, if you are called to). What I am suggesting is that by truly allowing myself to be in the process of my life – by not forcing, not pushing, and in this case showing up to my creativity, I crafted something that changed me.

I once worked with this amazing man, I'll call Ed. He was very senior at a large firm. He had a great wife and two fab kids. He came to me because he wanted to shift how he was seen around the business. He was known as the quiet leader – and he was happy with that to a point, yet he knew that he had more to give and wanted to find the courage to express it. In order to help him I had to first get him to reflect on when he'd ever liked how he'd shown up, and also on where he was not so keen on how he'd appeared. I also asked him to observe when he felt he was the best of himself at home or at work.

In essence I was getting him to look at how he was being present in his life. What emerged were patterns of less conscious awareness. He could see how some of his life had resulted from auto pilot mode. He was just coasting in some interactions. He realised there was not enough actual time for thinking and reflecting in his life. He observed that parts of how he had become successful had resulted in life getting "too busy". So, when he went home, he was processing and wanting thinking time and that was also having an impact on how he was at home.

He explored with me that this existing without consciously Being Present meant he was also always seeking outcomes in meetings. There was never any space for issues to be explored fully so as a result there were lots of quick wins but no long-standing solutions and fundamental changes.

In Cal Newport's *Deep Work* he describes a company that closes for a month from all client interaction and non deep work:

"The Company gave its employees the entire month of June off to work deeply on their own projects. This month would be free of any shallow work obligations – no status meetings, no memos and blessedly no PowerPoint. At the end of the month the company held a "pitch day" Where employees 1pitched their ideas they had been working on Summarising the experiment in an Inc magazine article Fried (the MD) dubbed it a success. The pitch day produced two projects that were soon put into production. These projects are predicted to bring substantial value to the company but they would have almost certainly not been produced in the absence of unobstructed deep work time provided to the employees. To tease out their potential required dozens of unimpeded effort."[4]

"How can we afford to put our business on hold to "mess around" with new ideas," Fried asked rhetorically.

"How can we not afford to?"

This example is a clear case for allowing yourself to be in your process in business. I am suggesting that you allow yourself to do this in your whole life not just your work life.

To Be Present in your own life will change you. It will help you create better boundaries. To address your true feelings and to show up to your life as you want to. When you are doing that you are allowing yourself to feel the feelings – as I have learnt to experience true joy, you have to allow yourself the potential to experience truly shitty things too.

That very moment. That spark. This moment. That is all there is. It is wonderful. You are wonderful right now. At the heart of each of us is a place of beauty and joy and wonderment. It is a place that is always there I am so lucky I know this.

I am no longer observing myself wearing a lot of different masks. I am no longer in the place of fear that my worst emotions will destroy me. I am no longer in fear of being seen as all of me. I am no longer in fear of any judgement because only I can judge me and why would I judge when I can just be who I always have been.

Life is a process. We all view success through different lenses. I know that by allowing myself to be present I am not letting fear and my fears dictate the life I want to have and how I want to show up.

If there was one final piece of evidence for that then it is this: You are reading a book written by me which is a testament to allowing myself to be in The Present.

In my adult life I have had so much fear of the written word; that I could not write. Most of this comes from school and not being diagnosed with dyslexia (God, that word is so cruel and kind of funny all at the same time). My self-doubting and self-deprecating belief about writing got bigger and bigger and I spent a lot of time avoiding writing.

With space, with allowing me to be in process, the possibility of me writing a book just emerged.

There is a whole lot of emerging in this book, hey!

I wonder: What will you allow when you allow yourself to fully be present?

What will you do that makes your heart sing when you allow yourself the space to shine the light on your brilliance? I wonder what other kind of fruits you have in your back pocket that are just bursting to be part of your fruit salad? [Aside: Warning: I mean if they are in your back pocket be careful, fruits can be messy!! I know easy gag … could not resist!]

Be Present.

Trust it.

Allow it.

Be conscious.

Breathe.

Reflect.

Your life will only get fuller and more abundant in every way. To do that you have to be in place where you are willing to take the next lesson on.

Be Accepting …

LESSON 4

BE ACCEPTING

ORANGE'S OFFERS FOR YOU

Use a "Yes And" or "Yes How" mindset not "Yes but".

Really listen to yourself.

Trust your inner voices are looking after you.

FADE IN:

EM STROUD enters wearing a black tee shirt with some weird arty farty logo on it. The audience is unsure what it is but are too polite to heckle. EM has silver and black trainers on that are made in Sweden. *(The sole is made of wood! Weirdly comfortable, in case you are wondering.)*

EM

Ah … gotta love it. What, Em? We've come this far together and now you're asking us to actually accept ourselves? What a ridiculous idea. I mean, as far as you're concerned, there is something wrong with you, am I right? I mean, you could not possibly accept yourself as you are. In your eyes, you're always too something: too thin, large, short, tall, weird stomached. You're not funny, you're too serious, quiet, loud, messed up, sorted. (Is there such a thing? Better include that in case that's how you beat yourself up.) You think you're too American, too French, too ... well, you get the idea. I mean you are, after all, so good at making sure that you always have something to beat yourself up with – sometimes it's not even these things already listed. No, sometimes it's deeper stuff such as I'm not confident, people think I'm too confident, I'm depressed, I'm not depressed, I'm creative but never earn any money. I am, well, just basically a bit shit. Ah … ya gotta to love us humans.

As I look at my dog Charlie (he is little, a pug, Jack Russell with a bit of chihuahua) he does not spend his time going, oh I wish my nose was bigger, or I was taller. Charlie just lives. He gets on. He ... yes, I am comparing all of us (me included) to the simplicity and acceptance that all other mammals have. I mean if we are so smart how come we are the only ones that beat ourselves up with inner chatter so much – maybe, just maybe, we aren't so clever after all!

Plus, Charlie never has to do any washing up ...

When I see anything or anyone. I get so excited. As I know they are perfect just as they are. I know that when I look what i see is already so beautiful. So fun. So joyous.

This is all well and good for Orange, but Fuck Me, I am not always very good at this whole accepting lark. I hope you are with me on this!! I have worked with so many people who fight their gifts, struggle with their genius and who at their heart don't feel they have anything to offer.

I so get it. So, what do we do about it?

We start to say "Yes and" to ourselves and we start to really listen to who we are. We start to see the good in us, not just all the bad bits. We start to become our own cheerleader.

Clowning and the whole art of performing require having a big mirror pointed at you.

Do you walk towards it or do you run away?

To be accepting of ourselves, a big mental reposition has to happen. I know that I could not have written this chapter for you two years, or even six months ago. Of all the lessons, this is the one I found the most difficult to convey. Knowing that I am perfectly okay at this moment and knowing that I am living my best life, is like ripping up of all the manuals that I so perfectly crafted when I was younger. It is false beliefs about ourselves that stop us from being accepting of who we are, and that is the biggest gift we can ever give ourselves.

It took me finding Orange to really grasp self-acceptance. Orange only ever says "Yes, and". Whatever space Orange is exploring – a rehearsal room, a show, or the world as I occasionally am out as Orange – all is possible.. Orange has the strongest driver of "Yes, and" as that opens up all possibilities and to allow that mindset Orange truly and deeply listens. Orange listens with no fear about what will be heard either from both Orange as Orange and indeed from the rest of the world.

Improvising and the beliefs around it are a useful metaphor (and as the skills required for acceptance are at the heart of improvising it seems wise to explore this now!) Many, many people that I have worked with believe that they cannot improvise.

I just did a gig for the Lean In Supper Club in London – (though this being COVID times it was on Zoom and it had a global audience.) When I asked the question, 'How many of you believe you can improvise?" in addition I asked them to put it on a scale of 1 to 10 with 1 being I can't at all and 10 being I love it. Ninety percent of the answers were between 1 and 3. I believe this is really about lack of self-trust.

This is what one of the people that attended this gig said:

What an amazing workshop with Em Stroud last night!

Em spoke about how we can use improv in business to deliver messages and lead with more confidence and engagement. Whilst preparation is ALWAYS important, you can't plan everything so you'll have to use improv even if you don't know it.

Three key steps:

1. Be present: Take a moment to pause and breathe, this helps you to feel calmer and more in control.

2. Listen: Practise active listening in all situations.

3. Move from yes … but to yes … how: Play, look for the opportunities instead of the restrictions.

Some other thoughts we loved:

- *Truly extraordinary people allow themselves to be fully themselves at home AND at work.*
- *Improv is about trusting yourself and that you have the right answer inside you.*
- *Show your vulnerability, bring your whole self to work and others will do the same.*

- *Play isn't just for the pub on Friday night. Bring it into your everyday work life and others will follow suit. People having a good time at work is good for morale and good for business.*
- *You can still have a serious conversation wearing a silly hat.*

It never fails to amaze me. It was Orange who got me to a place where I could share these lessons with others. I seriously never felt I would be able to be a Clown in business. I could never be a funny person who wanted so much more than just being the funny one, I thought. I wanted to make an impact and knew I could, yet I was too scared because I would have to bring all the parts of me, all of the fruits, out in public view. I didn't think I'd ever NOT be concerned about others' perceptions of me.

I have stopped blocking myself. In improvisation we use the phrase – don't block – this is where another player, (or indeed yourself) comes up with an idea and it is met with a "yes but" type of answer. Such as:

Two improvisers are playing a scene on a bus stop. The dialogue has been this standard:

"What time is the bus coming?"

"Think it's here in ten minutes."

"Oh great, thank you."

So far pretty standard dialogue, then player one does this:

"Look at that bat flying over there."

Player one is offering a new idea, the bat is a new concept in scene.

"I don't see any bat."

Player two has completely blocked the scene from going somewhere new. Blocking the idea will kill the scene.

Blocking shows that we have made our minds up, or we think we know what someone else is already going to give us. I know it happens a lot in the world of work – there are some people who decided in advance not to listen to ideas that come from others, because they have an agenda of their own to push. You know the kind. People don't feel expansive when their thoughts are not heard.

I was doing coaching work with a recent graduate years ago, who I'll call Fiona. She was super bright and keen to do well in her new role. Her boss told me that this young woman's challenge was that she never spoke up in meetings and it was holding her development within the company. I asked Fiona what was happening in meetings at work …

'I have these ideas and I want to contribute – but then I think, well that is probably a stupid idea and then I think about it a bit longer and decide I should say it – but by that point either we have moved on in the meeting or more annoyingly someone else says what I was already thinking.'

This is a classic way of blocking ourselves. Fiona's fear was about others. She created her own, "Yes but …" scenario and she ran with it. She was thinking the worst, not being accepting, and therefore not accepting herself and her ideas. No, not everything that you want to say will be brilliant! However, if we allow ourselves to speak up then others can build on these ideas – this gives us all something to work with rather than just blocking our own ideas. These blocks – this fear can come from many places. Our beliefs around ourselves come from many places and different voices – old teachers, parents, family members.

I did an in person gig last week (my first one since lockdown and it felt great!) one of the people that attended said – 'I have to be honest when I saw you, the topic, and how happy you looked, I thought I was going to hate it, I was trying to work out a way to not attend, but it's been brilliant.)

I wonder: How many times have you blocked yourself from exploring things that are not in your comfort zone?

How would it feel if you accepted yourself in all these situations and embraced the uncertainty?

Whose voice are you hearing in your head when you hesitate to accept yourself?

I teach and talk about impro and its skills all around the world. I truly love it and it still baffles me why people have so much fear it.

The heart of impro is rooted in three skills:

Be present, which as you know means breathing and being conscious about your intent

Listen

Accept all offers by having a Yes, And attitude

On the podcast I was talking to a fellow improviser who happens to be an academic too, Clay Drinko. We chat all things Play Yourself Sane and we explored more of how impro can really help us in our lives. His book *Play Your Way Sane* is full of great ways to use games in everyday activities. I love it when I get to chat to people who are passionate about using these skills in the non impro or theatre world. It's so gratifying that something I've spent 20 years learning makes a difference to people.

I was running a workshop with a group of CEOs and they were fearful. (I did not have to mind read this one, they told me!) The main fears were expressed in these ways:

'I'm not funny.'

'I'm not very good under pressure.'

'I'm not creative.'

'I hate this stuff.'

These and the like are very typical. I want to disassemble some of the fiction around improvisation.

Impro is a series of skills within itself – at the core of those skills are the three I have listed. I said skills, right? Because what I often see from people before experiencing impro is the expectation that we should be good at this naturally. This is the equivalent of saying you should be naturally good at plumbing … no one would expect you to be naturally great at that. Impro is an art form to be explored and experimented with. When

I direct an impro show I always say if we get 80 percent of a show then we have done exceptionally well. Have that in the back of your mind as we move forward with this! Trust me when I say I have done shows where only 30 percent has been good – and that is okay too. We accept that in the impro world. That to me feels like an achievable thing to aim towards acceptance too. One other piece to straighten out, while we are here. It is a mistake to liken improv to winging it. Winging it is bluster, arrogance, and occasionally fear mixed into a world of non-trust and non-acceptance. Impro allows you to access your knowledge and your wisdom. Skills will help you in those moments of pressure when you use this at work like when you need to answer questions that you had not prepped for in an interview. However, with all skills they need to be developed and practiced.

With that, how is the breathing going? ☺

Just checking…!

Know that if you are conscious about how you choose to show up, with a whole lot of preparation in what you are delivering, you will be brilliant.

Remember the listening part. To accept ourselves with our flaws our fears as well as our brilliance we have to listen to ourselves. I avoided this liberally! I think starting to accept me as me happened when I challenged myself to do Vipassana, a type of meditation that you learn by going on retreat for ten days. These ten days are also held in complete silence. No reading. No writing. No exercising. Just walking and meditation mixed in with a few lentils. I am not a fan of lentils … so that within itself was tricky. No eye contact. No engagement with anyone else.

(You can, of course, check in with your teacher if you are struggling and every other day, they do look at you to check in. You nod that you are okay. Plus, you can talk to one of the helpers if you need something, but they try to advise you to keep the human contact to the absolute minimum.)

So, silence.

I had been curious about Vipassana as some of the people in my world had done it. I would look at the website again and again and conclude, no. I didn't think I could do it. Then I signed up.

On the journey to the retreat, I was terrified. I did not go there with some massive agenda. I was just curious about what would happen and how I would respond. After the first few days I started to truly accept what was going on. I was able to be in the moment with the daily routine of rituals. (The bell rang at 430 am and again at 9 pm for the start and end of the day. There were ten hours of meditation and some time to eat more types of lentils than I knew existed! Oh, the day they brought out a baked potato and cheese was joyous (internal joy, mind you, as I could not share it with anyone).

I was not expecting what came up for me at this retreat.

In my twenties I had made the decision to never have kids. I was lucky enough to be a "mother" figure in my nephews' worlds and I had decided being a treasured aunt was enough for me. I recognised that my resistance to motherhood also had something to do not wanting to risk carrying on the cycle that I had learnt from my mother and that I had sadly witnessed in my sister also. When I was silent, when all the noise stopped from the world, I could really hear myself. (After all, there was nothing else to listen to!) One night I went into myself, and I had an overwhelming desire to write the names of a child for each letter of the alphabet.

Now pens etc were not allowed but my roommate had left a pen out ... I had a box of Tampax and I kid you not, I hid under my sheet with my torch (you were allowed that so you could go to the loo, as it is very dark there), and even though I felt as if I was committing a heinous crime I wrote a list of 26 girl names and 26 boy names. My heart slowed down. I sat crossed legged and stared at this illicit list and I knew my life would never be the same. I had accepted something from deep within me.

This was not completely out of the blue. My dear friend Deon had already spoken to me about us having a child together, and co-parenting and raising a child in our own gay clan. However, when Deon first asked me what my thoughts were, I completely shut it down with a hard no.

I knew the offer was still there though. I had been so fearful of what it could mean that I blocked it. As I sat there under my comforter with the torch shining on bed two lists of names, I had s allowed myself to listen and accept a new course.

I wonder: If you allowed yourself to really listen to yourself, what blocks could you move past?

In developing this as a practice and a skill these are the things that I have noticed:

I have stopped always pushing at things to get an outcome

I am learning that not all of my inner voices are cruel. (Yet, we are still a work in progress on that front, aren't we?)

I am better set up to help others when I listen to what I really want and articulate that. Speaking up and being brave comes from that knowledge of your own truth.

There is bravery required to accept ourselves fully.

We all have our pasts. We all have our beliefs about ourselves which are normally created by our experiences of when we were younger. I am often struck by how many people I have worked with who struggle with imposter syndrome, a perceived lack of confidence, a fear of challenging themselves, or even an resignation that life is always going to be a certain way. These are rocket fuel for self-blocking.

We must be brave and explore where these things come from and then we can make choice.

The biggest challenge? Acceptance.

Once on a walk through London I stopped at this shop and I met the most marvelous woman. She was so helpful. As I stood there looking for my new trousers to match my orange jacket she asked:

"What size are you dear?"

"I'm whatever size you make of me."

She laughed which I found a little odd but went off and found me these fabulous grey knit trousers. They were amazing. As she was of course.

As I've mentioned, I have never accepted my body. I have always found flaws in it and judged it too small, short, fat, and horrible stomach. My legs are okay, but they are so white. (You don't need a torch when you're with me and my bare legs.)

In that shop, I had allowed myself to be Orange and I left with what in Orange's mind are the most amazing trousers for Orange. The world of what a Clown wears could be a whole book, too. To summarise, a Clown will always believe that they look amazing, they always wear clothes that at first glance appear fine, and perfectly normal. But upon closer inspection something will be not quite right – patterns that do not quite go together, slightly wrong sizes, etc. In Orange's case, Orange likes to wear these horrible grey tweed trousers, with an over large puffy orange jacket with pockets, a white shirt with braces and a hat. Orange feels amazing in this. As Em would I wear this, hell no! You've read the bits in this book where I'm always in black, the tie, the trainers, etc.

As I left Orange and came back into Em, I realised that for those moments in this shop I had stopped judging and disliking my body. I had accepted me.

I wonder: What it would take for you to really accept all of you?

Is it possible that you do not need to be fixed or that you are exactly as you are meant to be and that is just wonderful?

HOW DO WE DO THIS MAGICAL MINDSET SHIFT?

To get to this place of acceptance, you need mindset change. [Aside: What after all this build up you have to actually change how you think? 'Can't I just take a pill, Em', you're thinking.] Part of my journey was paying attention to what I had been helping thousands of people do: create awareness of the "Yes And" versus the "Yes But" mentality and in some cases the "Yes How" mindset.

I often ask rooms of people how they feel when people block their ideas? The response is that they don't feel valued, they don't want to speak up again, they feel stupid, etc. I am sure here you could add your own. The challenge is that not only do we often get those type of responses from others, we hear the dialogue internally too.

I wonder: Do you hear any of these voices in your head?

Don't say it in case it's wrong

They will think this isn't a great idea

What happens if I do say that and they all laugh at me

What if this is not a perfectly formed idea yet

And many more. To accept ourselves, we must confront these internal narratives.

We have to listen, and we also need to recognise how we speak to ourselves. For so long I was so scared of owning who I truly was. This book writing thing, acknowledging my place in the world is perhaps one of the biggest pieces of acceptance I have ever done. The understanding that I have something of value and that I can own the space between Clown, coach, performer, speaker and most importantly, human. My voice as I have written this has been full of the internal voice of "Yes But" … the dialogue goes like this.

If I write this then people will finally hear my truth. Yes but no one gives a shit.

If I am brave and share what I have learnt it might help people. Yes, but you are still in therapy so what do you know about being happy and fully content as a human?

If you finally write this then the new chapter of your life will have a solid launching pad. Yes, but it is unlikely to ever be sold.

You get the idea. I have had to look at all these and accept them and the manner that I have done this has been using the "Yes How" mindset. Going from a "Yes But" to a "Yes And" is too large a leap. I know I will perhaps get there, but first I have taken these steps … hence you are reading this!

In the second draft of Lessons from a Clown I used the "Yes How" mindset to accept that I do have these negative voices, that I am fearful, and then I gently moved my thinking along. If you are in a situation where you are always with someone who uses a "Yes But" attitude as yourself what difference it could make if you asked them to try "Yes How".

I wonder: How would it feel if you allowed yourself to try having a "Yes How" attitude.

I was working with Helen who is a director of a mid-sized firm. She and I discussed how she was being seen on the senior leadership team. Her main concern was that she was always seen somewhat negatively. She believed part of being a good financial director was to be the prudent voice of reason. (Her company was a creative agency and she sometimes felt isolated as her way of thinking was very different to every else on this team.) I pushed Helen to observe herself using the feedforward method. She noticed that there were certain people that she felt did didn't always make the best decisions who she was quite "Yes But" towards. I asked her to show up with a "Yes How" attitude in the next interaction and note how she felt.

She was astounded by how this simple act changed the energy in meetings. When she responded with a "Yes How" attitude, encouraging the person to elaborate on their idea explore their thinking they often came to the Helen's conclusion, that it was not a great idea. Although this was a great result from her perspective the bonus was that it made her happy.

I always want to know what is going on, behind peoples' eyes and faces there are so many stories – so many possibilities and isn't that a wonderful place to explore. It is a place of magic where all is possible.

The stories that we tell ourselves, that form our narrative, say much to me about how accepting (or unaccepting) we are of ourselves. I often ask the questions that no one else does ... I want to know who they really are. I think this makes me a good coach. With the questions also comes the requirement to accept what we hear as responses at any given time. Sometimes stories are too much or too hard to share and I know that ...

Before I met Orange when I was doing my Coming Out of My Box Show there were some stories that felt too much or too big to share yet. Part of my path was also learning to accept that. One of the ways that I made myself feel safe and accept where I was is by using this very simple model.

HAPPY TO TELL	WOULD LIKE TO TELL	KEEP TO SELF

Underneath each heading I would put a trigger word, so I knew the stories that I was willing to share and those that were not quite ready and those that felt I would not ever share. I often suggest that clients who are looking to work out what stories they want to put in keynotes use this method. It's a good way of connecting with where you are at. It is good and useful to accept where you are at right now.

Understand that this is likely to change. For Coming Out of My Box I kept to myself the stories of my suicidal thoughts that I have had throughout my life. By the time I wrote my second one woman show called *Re:Framed* I chose to include the scene where I was standing on a platform noticing the Samaritans sign and making the decision to step back. I've gone even further now, choosing to include this in my film and extending support to the Samaritans and their work.

Over time I have learned to accept and be kind to myself about these times and tell the stories that are my truth. In fact, it was Orange who set the scene by getting the whole audience in my show to become a train in a very light comic manner.

> I loved it getting the whole audience on one side to go "chugga chugga" and the other side to go "choo choo" was brilliant! They loved it! I loved it! The energy was amazing.

It *was* remarkable. That moment also allowed a change of mood to take the audience on a journey, and Orange allowed me the space to hold that story. Orange shows me time and again that light always accompanies darkness.

I continue to breathe into this place of acceptance. By accepting ourselves as all who we really are, by listening to ourselves, by accepting our own offers and insights, by accepting all of what makes us who we are – that is where the magic lies. I am learning is a magical pot of energy that fuels expansion.

As I sat with the torch looking at my list of names, I was accepting what was coming next –the greatest adventure of my life. I became a mother to a boy named William. (Yes, that was the W on my boy name list). With William and Orange around I can do nothing but embrace the final lesson from them both. It is now time to Be Playful.

LESSON 5

BE PLAYFUL

ORANGE'S OFFERS FOR YOU

Play connects us to joy.

Play allows us to be free.

Play is a state of mind that can take you away from the current state of the world.

FADE IN:

EM STROUD is seated in her home office. She turns on her screen and accepts the hundreds of people into her online gig. She is wearing a full jester costume. She sees all their faces light up as they see her. *(When they see a jester on a Zoom call, they know it is going to be a good meeting!)*

EM

I hear you.

What, me? Play?

Don't be ridiculous – I stopped playing a long time ago. Afterall, play is what kids do, right?

No way do I want to look silly in front of other people. I mean, I have a professional job. I'm a parent. I'm a proper, fully-carded adult with all the things that come with being a grown up, bona fide big person.

Play is just fine for me though, isn't it? I'm a Clown. So that's allowed. And you like it when others play, because you have to admit, that makes the world more fun. But you're not going to play, are you? No way. You're far too busy to waste your time on something childish.

Who cares that it makes you feel good and that you like smiling and laughing? You're far too busy for that kind of behaviour.

Come on, Em … why don’t you just grow up?

That’s you, right? Or at least a part of you. I mean the idea of play sounds okay if it’s in the pub. That’s when you can play.

When did we all become so, well, scared of allowing the good times in so we might just be happy?

There are so many games I love! I love the one where we have to creep up to someone who is sitting on a chair and there are loads of things around it and we have to get them without them the person pointing at us. We have to get all the things ... like keys, bottles, all kinds of stuff, and not be got! The person on the chair has a blindfold on. So, they have to be soooo into their listening ... I love it. Creep, creep, and then get all the things back to our end of the room. It is brilliant. We have a time limit sometimes – it is brilliant.

I love the game of smiling too – that is a game I play when no one else knows that I am playing! It is the game of seeing how many people I can get to smile by smiling at them. Sometimes it takes so long! But when I do get them to smile, it's the best feeling ever!

I used to fear playing. I always wanted to play but I would talk myself out of it. I thought that I had to behave like an adult and that meant play wasn't open to me. It took me reconnecting with Clowning to really remember how to play and live a playful life. Just yesterday I was doing a gig in Yorkshire. I started off talking about how I believe that levity – the lightness in our hearts – is so needed right now. I went on to explain that the only way that levity will become more integrated into our lives is by us allowing ourselves to play. Right. Now. I felt some fear talking about play in this way. I looked at those attentive faces, and I knew there were sceptical adults looking back me. I knew they were up against some of the same blocks that I had confronted myself.

I asked them to share some of the resistant thoughts that were coming up for them.

Do you recognise yourself in any of these?

- *I don't really know how to play.*
- *I don't have time to play.*
- *Play is not for me in work.*
- *Play and business don't go together. I'm a _______ lawyer, teacher, coach, or insert any grown-up title.) Sure, I understand playing with the kids, but even with them I quite often say 'I don't have the time'.*

I thanked them for sharing and then offered three statements. How do these land with you?

Play is the simplest act of love you can do for yourself; as it frees you from your head and connects you to your heart.

Play allows you to explore who you really are, not who you think you are.

Play allows you to be brave and curious in new worlds; it is through play that we truly learn.

I looked out at the faces again. I sensed that they had were feeling less resistant. Perhaps they hadn't thought of play in this way. Maybe they were seeing that play wasn't just kids' stuff. We began to play some games and by the end of the gig they were doing things they never expected to like throw imaginary balls around. All fun and joyful stuff! Many attendees told me that playing had shifted their thinking in a way they were surprised by. It had opened their eyes to "how" they were showing up in their everyday lives, not only (as this was a gig for a business) at work, but also at home. I understood where they were coming from. They thought that play was a thing to do. But I see it as allowing the opening of our hearts to receive and accept joy.

My own challenge of play …

This was really put to the test recently when I had a tough weekend. You know the kind I'm talking about, where loads of stuff is happening around you. It's not about you; it's about people you care about and are close to. A dear friend of mine was admitted into hospital. He will be okay, but it was scary. On the same day someone very close in my family had a serious mental health crisis. This was an intense weekend for me, as I love both people a lot. During a time that could have been unbearably stressful, I found myself playing a game with my partner and my son. It was child led, but we all went with it. The game involved table tennis balls and drinking glasses and the consuming of horrible drinks by the one who did not get the ball in the glass. The drinks were gross. Coffee and soda water, (which was disgusting!) Lime cordial with milk ... you get the idea. We played this game for nearly an hour.

Did the adult stuff go away? No.

Did it change the reality of what was happening to those I care about? No.

What it did do was allow all of us to come together and have a different shared experience that we talked about for the rest of the night. And we giggled and laughed. In that time of worry and fear, it was so important for me to remember that laughter was as true as anything else. It was the playing that kept us all together.

We find the time to work. Why do we not find the time to play?

Sometimes we play a game where loads of us have to keep a ball up in the air for as long as possible – when we start this game, we are normally really pleased to get to ten or twenty. This is not good! As we are playing this all of us are still in our adult brain – deciding, I'm no good at ball sports, or (in Em's case) I'm good at ball sports – so everyone takes the role their adult self has. Then I take over – the joy comes from playing the game, from passing the ball to one person and knowing that there will be times when the ball will be nowhere near you – the others have it – you are in the game, and you can enjoy others being in the game ... when I was in charge with others then we got to over 1000!

Thinking back to Clown school again.

This game. This game. For the first two mornings of playing this game we were so shit. And all of us that thought we were "good" at sports had the responsibility in our minds of helping those that were not good at ball sports. Then De Castro reminded us that it's about playing, and it's about being. It's about passing the ball to one person and finding the joy just in that. That discovery made the shift in me. We needed just to be in the moment. I found myself slowing down and enjoying it when others were playing, and the ball was on the other side of the room. Enjoying and living every moment of the game – yes, being fully present and somehow, even more than that – it was being free.

Now you might not find yourself in a room of clowns with a teacher who is sharing these words. This was part of our deep practice of changing our state. However, I know that we can all feel this freedom, these moments of joy that when combined, fuel our bodies with all the good stuff that will help us enjoy ourselves throughout life. Which is surely why we are here, isn't it? To live and have fun and feel alive? I know that when I play, I feel most alive. It is just waiting there for us to access.

Some of you may be responding that you don't want to get your shoes dirty or mess up your hair, etc., and that's okay.

I wonder: What would happen if you allowed yourself to play?

Play for each of us is different.

Let's go back to the nursery. (You remember all the little people playing in different ways …)

Some building blocks into towers. Some building blocks into towers and knocking them over.

The list is endless. For me the key here is that it is all play. Each little person in their playing time will do what they are most interested in. Play is a conscious choice.

When people ask me: How do I play more? I always have to be a politician and say I don't know, how do you play?

WHAT DOES PLAY LOOK LIKE FOR YOU?

Take this moment to breathe and put the book down. In your notebook maybe you could write a list of what kinds of things look and feel like play for you.

There is no wrong answer here.

Here are some ideas to get you started. These appeared in the Psychologies Magazine in an article I wrote with Dr Mandy Lehto (love her work, check her out!)

- Spend 5 min learning to juggle (find a YouTube tutorial).
- Doodle for two minutes in your journal.
- Throw a dry tea bag into a cup from one meter away.
- Kitchen dance to your favourite song while making brekkie. (I did this to a Tina Turner song last week – loved it!!)
- Skip for at least 15 seconds on your walk. *(Try doing it when no one is looking and then next time try doing it when someone is!)*
- Buy a toy you really want. Puzzle? Rubik's cube?
- Wear only items that begin with the letter P or D today.
- Make a spaceship out of foil - or doodle a rocket.
- Build a den in a park (or in your house). Great with kids!
- Add a fun colour to your hair, or style it differently. Or try a hat.
- Write a story in five minutes – make it silly!
- Watch your favourite comedian on YouTube and giggle.
- Drink an ice cream shake or eat a chocolate bar you loved as a kid.
- Read a fun book for 10 to 15 minutes that's not related to work.
- Play a card game (or a board game).
- Get some Blu Tack or Play Doh and make into something cool in 5 minutes.

- Send a silly voice note to a friend – just because …
- Create an obstacle course in your house or garden.
- Draw a monster and be abstract – snakes with socks, etc …
- Place an item that feels playful on your desk.
- Get dressed in the dark, putting on what you touch first.
- Create an ice block skyscraper. How high can you build it?

Once I did a speaking gig and for a group of people working within a service industry. There was a mix of people from directors to the newest intern. The aim of the gig was to give them all a boost, as their industry had been impacted by the COVID pandemic. I asked: What does play mean to you? I got a variety of responses from being silly, something I do with the kids, to something I do not do. When I asked a few more questions I discovered they felt fear about getting play right – and also that play was not allowed in their very structured days. We then played some games and I shared ideas from the list above. I asked how they felt after. They all said they felt happier, more relaxed, and more present. One woman said her child often asks her to play and she always responds that she is too busy. She said that she intended to change that because her too busy was really only about being on her phone.

I wonder: Do think that you don't have time to play?

What if you allowed yourself the time? How would your life feel?

I mean, how might you feel? As I write, I can't help but smile at these ideas and having done all of them I know how they make me feel. Yet some of you might be reading this and thinking, 'I don't have time for play. I'm too busy'. Could it be that some adult part of you that dismisses play as a waste of time, or as being superfluous to your life? Have years of conditioning led you to repeat this belief to yourself?

I worked with a client who said accessing his playfulness was difficult because he was conditioned to be so adult. Keith started to consciously allow himself to embrace his childlike parts and a few months later he said he felt lighter, happier and had noticed he was far less stressed. I have yet to meet one person this isn't true for.

This was put to the test once when I did a speaking gig to a room of lawyers in the UK. The organisation had asked me to come in and provide something different for their group. They were the partners and managing partners of the most renowned law firms, an audience of sharp minds and quick dismissals. I knew it was an opportunity for me to put this Be Playful lesson to the test.

I had to bring my best. I knew that there was every chance that I would leave this gig with either the best or the worst testimonial of my speaking. I felt the fear. Before the gig I had to get myself into the right state. I decided on my intent and wrote my simple notecard words – fun, engage, curious. I was near the river Thames and there was this cool little park near the venue. It was starting to get dark, and it was as if winter was knocking on the door. I got them myself to that park. I took time to breathe.

(Remember that? You doing it? Just checking!)

I breathed. I then cranked some tunes and with my headphones on I let Orange in …

We sang and danced around the park – not big dancing but we danced, and I saw and noticed all the little things in the park. We played silly songs, bit songs, and inspiring songs. We had so much fun.

I checked in on me and then went into the venue.

Yip, posh. Check.

Yip, lots of champagne already flowing. Check.

Yip, a very friendly, if slightly fierce, lady introduced me and she wore more pearls than I had ever seen around one person's neck. Check.

I took to the floor … over 30 of the top legal minds in London stared back at me. *Holy fuck. Breathe.*

They were all staring at me intently with what I perceived was a mix of slight disinterest, vague curiosity, and a ton of ambivalence. *Oh joy. All I can do is control me. All I am in charge of is me. So, I play. So, I trust.*

I played. I told them a story. I told them all about being a banana. I told them about putting on masks. I told them and showed them who I was and delivered the story with the ease of muscle memory – they laughed, sipped their expensive champagne, and visibly relaxed as I pulled them into my world. I moved around the stage, telling the story through all of me, with Orange popping up here and there commenting.

They opened up.

The laughing changed the space.

Then the big moment.

This transaction had all been fine. As I was there to entertain to engage, what they did not know is that they are also going to have to join in this. And not just by engaging with me but by engaging with each other through play. I felt it – I had won most of them over.

Then I said, 'Right, it's your turn.'

The room changed. The energy ran cold. *Fuck it, I've started, gotta trust.*

'Yip, all of you are coming with me." (I had another room empty and ready to go)

They all reluctantly followed me, with the groans and gripes of an audience who believed they were there to be observers, not participants. We moved into the opulent room with a chandelier hanging in the middle. It swung gently and I noted that if this all went to shit maybe I could swing out on it.

'Get in a circle, we're going to play zoof.'

If you are reading this and have ever played any impro games then you might know it as zip, zap, bong. The version I like to play is zoof. Which includes the words – Zoof, Back, Wee, Shazam, and Ha. Each of these words signify a way that energy can be passed around the circle. Zoof is to the person next to you, Back then deflects that, Shazam is across the circle, Ha deflects that, and Wee is over someone else's head.

As I write that I realise how absurd it sounds. Trust me it is a great game, one that engages groups in eye contact, being present, and so much more. However, as I stood in the middle of the room with the chandelier above me I did wonder if the fixture falling on me would be a useful distraction.

I taught them the game. I witnessed the following in the beginning:

Folded arms

Questioning heads

Moments of distraction through bits and bobs of conversation

Blocked body language

Then the game starts to do its magic … these postures started to disappear, giving way to laughter and giggles. Suddenly this room of well-educated, (if standoffish), legal minds became one teeming with people playing and shouting Ha! at one another. The game flowed, we mixed it up. We played for a few rounds until everyone was fully with me.

We then played other games:

We painted scenes of invisible films with invisible paint brushes, we then share these scenes with much wonder and awe with each other

We pulled items out of invisible boxes.

We threw invisible balls.

(No, not all my games are around invisibility!!)

We created stories one word at a time and then the play part for them was over.

"Time to go back to your drinks and the other room." They left chatting. The energy was bubbly and light. They assembled back as my audience, ready to fall into the compliant act of listening to me and sipping their drinks.

I looked at them and breathed. They were no longer a room of lawyers known for their positions, professional specialties, and high-profile clients and cases, they are fully connected humans that laughed, smiled, and engaged with me and each other. We chatted a bit about our experience, but I wasn't there as a learning facilitator. I was there to motivate them, entertain them, and remind them of their humanness.

I told them of my own experiences of lawyers and how I often witness them being put up on a pedestal, with higher status than too many others. I shared how hard I tried to not do that when I was preparing for the gig and yet, I still had.

The gig came to an end, and they applauded. I joined them for their dinner. (Although this was an after-dinner gig, we'd opted to do it pre-dinner before too much wine was consumed!) I sat with six of the audience members and faced a barrage of questions about the process and my feelings about what I do. I got the best testimonial. As I left, I noted that I felt so grounded by the experience. Sharing those games with that group had been just as significant for me as doing it with other Clowns, or performers. Play is the unifying element.

To play is to be human.

Take some time now and look at the list you have already created and go a bit deeper.

What does being playful mean to you?

How do you feel when you play?

What did you love to do when you were a child?

What excites you to play?

My list of play and what I love to do is below. I am sharing it with the hope that it acts as a guide for you.

HOW I PLAY:

- Impro
- Character discoveries
- Writing
- Sport
- Podcasting
- LEGO building
- Creating playlists on Spotify
- Guitar
- Using whiteboards
- Dancing in the kitchen
- Singing
- Doing weird stuff with my voice while driving
- In coaching
- Juggling
- Climbing

As I write my list I realise how much play is at the heart of what I do. When I moved house recently I got really fixated on the unpacking and

William just wanted to play. I kept saying to him, ‘Later’, ‘Later we will play water balloons,’ and then I took a moment and asked myself, what am I doing? We went out and we played and after that unpacking had a whole different energy.

I get that for you this list might not be what you want to do.

I wonder: How could play and playfulness change your life?

There is so much darkness in our world and so much heaviness that I believe adding playfulness into our lives is for the benefit of all of us. It is the part of our lives that brings us joy and makes us smile so why would you not want to include all of that. Being Playful is a conscious choice you can exercise at any time.

FINALE

I made a conscious choice recently, when William met Orange.

The experience of lockdown during the COVID-19 pandemic has impacted us all globally. As much as I love being playful, of course there are moments where even I've had enough. One day recently I'd reached my limit for playing football in the garden with William. William loves football. Loves it. Breathes it. During lockdown we played A LOT of football. A LOT. [Aside: I think it may have been a lot, dear reader … just in case you were unsure.] On this day we had already played for a good couple of hours, our allotted leave the house once per day for exercise. (Which I was so grateful for – I know how other countries did not even allow this.) William wanted to play some more.

My heart sank. I was done.

William knows what I do, to a certain extent. I mean let's be honest what 9-year-old really cares what their parent does? He knows that I make people laugh and he quite often tells me how I am not very good at that as I can't make him laugh on cue. (He is my toughest audience for sure. Lawyers, you are all forgiven!) Once when an optician asked William what I did for a living, he happily replied, "Oh my mum dresses up as a banana."

He likes getting the reaction. (No idea where he gets that from.)

He also knows that I do Clowning, and I am Clown. However, until this point of ever lasting football playing, I had never introduced Orange to William.

As he asked me to play more that day, I was about to say, 'I do not want to play anymore, I'm tired …'

I made a choice … I decided to let Orange out to play.

I LOVED IT. Every time William put some balls in one place I would then have to go and find them and no matter how quickly I seemed to move he was always one step ahead of me. We laughed. I got so confused I mean how did they keep moving, we giggled, I tried kicking the balls and I kept missing. Turns out I am not that great at football and we played and played ...

Until I realised it was time to make dinner. That hour was one of the most delicious of lockdown. In our back garden there is a step up from the house to the lawn. (When I say lawn, I mean really worn-down bit of old grass and dirt. It is not a massive space by any stretch of the imagination.

Instinctively I knew that when I went down the step I would be Em the mum again, not Orange. As I took the step and came back into the adult part of me, I turned and looked at William and asked what he wanted for dinner. He looked up and said fish fingers, chips, and peas. He then kicked the ball and as I went in, he followed me and asked:

'When you come back out will it be you or the silly you?'

'Oh, Orange you mean?'

'Yes, Orange.'

'Well, if you like, I think Orange would love to play some more if that's okay with you?'

'Yes, that's cool,' as he turned and resumed his goal kicking practice.

Somehow all my worlds had collided. Up until this point I was not sure how William would react to Orange, and if it would be, well, frankly just a bit weird for him, me being his mum and all. Turns out it was not weird, as he felt the heart of Orange. He knew that Orange just wants to play, only sees that moment, and finds joy in things that make William happy. Proof, if I needed it, that Orange is just as much part of me as any other part. William knew that.

I asked William if it would be alright with him if I wrote about this. I wondered how he remembered that day. He said it so well I wrote it down. 'Oh, you mean the time that you really played and were really silly and fun, when we played for ages, and you did not get bored of the game at all?'

Yip, that is what I meant.

Play more.

To play is to be human. To create joy and laughter is what pulls us all together. Allowing ourselves to laugh, create joy, and have moments of play is the deepest act of love that we can allow ourselves. Play allows us to try things, to fail, to succeed, to grow, and to be in the moment. Through play we can connect with each other and ourselves. That is the greatest act of courage.

Orange, thank you.

FADE IN:

EM STROUD enters the small and intimate space. The audience knows this is the end of the show. EM is dressed in black top, black trousers and wears her red DC trainers. She goes to the mic and takes it off the too high stand.

EM

Wow. So, we made it, hey? I mean that was a thing right there. Holy moley. And how good do you feel? And, breathe!! (Yip, still checking that you're doing that!) Right now, I'm feeling pretty darn good. That question … "Is this it …?" Remember that, all the way back at the start? You know, when we first met? It does seem like a life time ago. Now, I don't profess that this is you all done … of course not. Let's face it, life is just not like that, right? But as I stand here, I know one thing about life and living: We choose to turn on or turn off the spotlight in our lives. For me … I want mine to be on, so I can see myself and grow. Of course, mine is here on the stage and yours may not be - but I do know that if you let yourself shine then everything is possible. I mean this is proof of that, right? I am here on stage, in my book, that you have just finished. Before I take my bow, give yourself that moment of praise. Allow yourself that smile - yes, that one. You have got this.

Keep being you, all of you. As we all need you to do that. I'm going to pause now. So … until next time

Thank you.

And please.

Remember these Lessons from a Clown.

Lights down. EM exits the stage.

The curtain slowly closes.

ENDNOTES

1. "Clowning Explained" at www.ninalevine.com. http://www.ninalevine.com/clowning-explained.html
2. "A funny thing happened on the way to sociology: Goffman, Mills, and Berger" Patricia Cormack, James F Cosgrave, David Feltmate.

   First Published January 25, 2017. https://journals.sagepub.com/doi/10.1111/1467-954X.12421
3. Mark Lonergan Talks Benefits of Clowning by Lisa Jo Sagolla, for "Backstage". https://www.backstage.com/magazine/article/mark-lonergan-talks-benefits-clowning-59289
4. Cal Newport, Deep Work: Rules for Focused Work in a Distracted World. Grand Central Publishing, 2016. page 217.

ACKNOWLEDGEMENTS

There are many people that I want to thank and acknowledge.

Firstly, my thanks to you. That's right, you – all of you who are reading this book. Thank you for taking a leap and buying a book called *Lessons from a Clown*. Thank you, truly. I hope it has served you.

To my friends and the book's first readers, thank you so much for reading this book before release! Big love to you all: Sarah, Emily, Caroline, Kasia, Terri, Cag, Molly, Fred, Alana, David, Helen, Lisa, Katie, Mandy, Rob, Luc, Lucy, Maheen, Ramon, Izzy, Maisie, Stella, Shoshana, Lucinda, Rachel and Padideh. I am so grateful for you all, not only for reading my book but for all the love and care you show me.

To all my clients from my amazing mastermind folks to my corporate clients, to all my speaking and emcee and coaching clients, thank you for working with me and trusting me with your people – I hope this book can help you even more!!

There are some people without whom this book would not exist – Team Em – the individuals that helped me get to a place where I could write an actual book.

Firstly, Patti M Hall – What a woman you are! Without you this would never exist. For your kindness and skill, your wit and wisdom, I will always be so grateful; along with your friendship and care. I can never fully express my gratitude for your skill in helping me get this book into something I can be proud of. Fancy doing it all again? ☺

Dr Shoshana Garfield – Thank you for your kindness, patience, and expertise. Your ability to help me process my life has been crucial to me getting to a point that I could write a book. Thank you truly.

Dr Mandy Lehto – A long while ago you got a phone call from me. I wanted to ask you to be my coach, but I was too scared of what that would mean. You chose to pick up the phone and ring me back after I had waffled on at you. That phone call has changed my life. Working with you has helped me find the courage to write this book and find my voice. Thank you truly.

Ramon – What can I say about you? You make my world happen, you deal with me every day being me and you make it possible for me to do all the things I want to do. I am so lucky to have you in my world. You are a brilliant soul, and truly gifted at what you do. I can never say thank you enough.

Lucinda – You will hate this. (He He.) If you were not in my corner this book would not have happened. You have helped me for years, not only keeping my body moving, but your kindness you have always seen me and for that I am truly grateful.

De Castro – Thank you for helping me reconnect with Clowning and being a truly inspirational teacher.

Maheen – Thank you for being my collaborator for the last ten years and giving me the courage to tell my stories and share my voice. Bastille will always rock.

Thank you to Emee who is without a doubt the Amazon queen. Your expertise blows my mind, and I am so lucky that you came into my life!

Thank you to Dino. I mean, look at the book you made! Thank you for being such an amazing artist and fellow creator.

To the people who have featured in the book, from my podcast guests to those who are my clients I thank you all for being brave and working and talking with me.

Alana – Thank you for being you and coming into my life and making it so much richer in every way.

William – My boy, thank you for always reminding me to play and helping me be the best me I can be. You are amazing and I love you very much.

Deon and Annalea – Thank you for being the family I never had.

David, Mark and Darren – I know, I wrote a book! I'm shocked too! Love you all and never stop believing in yourselves.

Pam – Thank you for being you throughout my life.

Em Stroud is on a mission to get the world to laugh, think and play more. She can be seen emceeing and speaking at events across the world. She runs mastermind groups for CEOS, MDs and entrepreneurs. Clients include – Barclays, Bloomsburg, Bayer – to name a few (that all happen to start with a B!)

SOLO SHOWS

ME: EM

Me: Em explored identity and how Em has unmasked herself to work out who the hell she is. Expect giggles a plenty, a tear or two, and perhaps even some questions to make you think about who you really are and why that matters.

RE:FRAMED

Her current creative production is an autobiographical film called Re:Framed. This is a story of one woman and her challenges with identity, mental health, coming out and motherhood and how she found happiness. It will make audiences laugh and think. This has been adapted from her Me:Em. Re:Framed will be shown at conferences and for business, as well as available to the general public from 2022.

Watch the trailer here:

https://www.linkedin.com/in/emma-stroud/

CLOWNING AROUND PODCAST

Her podcast Clowning Around launched successfully in Feb 2020 and is now a Top 30 podcast in the UK with listeners worldwide.

Link to listen here:
https://emmastroud.london/clowning-around-podcast/

HIGHLIGHTS:

Dr. Gay Hendricks | Psychologist | Author | Teacher [Episode 87] had this to say about his episode with Em: *"I really enjoyed my conversation with Em Stroud and her clown posse. Humor is so important to enlightenment and healing. Good on ya, Em!"*

Martin Lindstrom | Founder and Chairman of Lindstrom Company | Speaker | Author of seven New York Times best-selling books including *Brand Sense*. Called one of the "World's 100 Most Influential People" by TIME Magazine. [Episode 54]

Gordana Biernat |Speaker | Thinker | Teacher| Member of Oprah's Super Soul 100 since 2016 | Author, *Know the Truth* [Episode 64]

Rajeeb Dey MBE | Entrepreneur | Founder and CEO of Learnerbly workplace learning platform| Young Global Leader to World Economic Forum since 2012. [Episode 59]

Vanessa Vallely OBE |Speaker | Author of the forthcoming, *Heels of Steel*| Founder and CEO, WeAreTheCity.com [Episode 13]

EPISODES THAT TOUCH ON LESSONS FROM A CLOWN CONTENT:

Clowning Around … Mindfulness with Louise Chester

https://podcasts.apple.com/gb/podcast/episode-74-clowning-around-mindfulness-with-louise/id1499174238?i=1000523781038

Clowning Around … Play Yourself Sane with Clay Drinko

https://podcasts.apple.com/gb/podcast/episode-65-clowning-around-play-yourself-sane-with/id1499174238?i=1000515023161

Clowning Around … Clowns Without Borders with Samantha Holdsworth

https://podcasts.apple.com/gb/podcast/episode-63-clowning-around-clowns-without-borders-with/id1499174238?i=1000513245108

Clowning Around … Mind Monsters with Hazel Gale

https://podcasts.apple.com/gb/podcast/episode-30-clowning-around-mind-monsters-with-hazel-gale/id1499174238?i=1000486382523

Clowning Around … Conscious Business with Padideh Tosti

https://podcasts.apple.com/gb/podcast/episode-25-clowning-around-conscious-business-with/id1499174238?i=1000479329943

Clowning Around … Comedy and Business with Julie Streets

https://podcasts.apple.com/gb/podcast/episode-81-clowning-around-comedy-and-business-with/id1499174238?i=1000529470640

Clowning Around ... Deep Coaching with Dr. Amina Aitsi-Selmi

https://podcasts.apple.com/gb/podcast/episode-11-clowning-around-deep-coaching-with-dr-amina/id1499174238?i=1000471440833

“From the moment Emma said “Hello” through to the moment she said “thank you for listening” the experience of being on Emma’s podcast was like no other I have been on (I’ve been on a lot). It was like being caught in a downpour of positivity, excitement, and wonderfully unexpected tangents without an umbrella. Emma’s way of engaging with the world is a joy and a real pleasure to be invited to be a part of.”

Steve Chapman ~ Artist. Clowning Around ... Silence with Steve Chapman, episode 49

https://clowningaroundthepodcast.libsyn.com/episode-49-clowning-around-silence-with-steve-chapman

ARTICLES

She writes regularly for various magazines including Psychologies Magazine, The Edge (Institute of Leadership and Management magazine) and Cosmopolitan, and has been a featured expert on the BBC and ITV.

SPEAKING

My TEDx talk "Be More Banana" is based on the idea that we all need to have more fun and joy in our lives. We all need to #bemorebanana! The talk's content stemmed from spending a day dressed as a banana going to an event in London and then meeting people around the city. I noticed that all people wanted to chat, to engage, and to smile while I was in costume. At the heart of our lives, I believe we all want to be happy and in order to do that we need to allow more fun and joy into our lives.

https://www.ted.com/talks/emma_stroud_bemorebanana_spreading_more_fun_and_joy_in_your_life

WORKING WITH EM

I love working with people who are open and brave and want to change their lives for the better. Every year I run two mastermind groups, each run for ten months. – I accept six people onto each mastermind group – we meet once a month for three hours and everyone that I invite to my Laugh. Think. Play mastermind group also gets four hours of one-on-one coaching time with me. In our hours together I help people go from being good to great or in some cases great to exceptional. We have a bucket load of fun and lives and businesses change.

In addition to my mastermind group, I work with a few individuals each year. If you are brave and curious and willing to change then this might be for you. I have worked on a one-to-one basis with people for over fifteen years and no one person is the same.

I work with organisations running Thinking Circles – short, intensive hours of group work sessions every other week for eight weeks. They work. They are brilliant. Maximum 8 people in each group.

I also run workshops and speak around the world on topics including – "Improvisation: a Vital Skill for Business Success", "Be the Best You", "Storytelling and You – create more impact", and "Lessons from a Clown – what the Clown can teach business leaders

WEBSITES

Emma Stroud Website:

https://emmastroud.london/

Laugh Think Play website:

https://laughthinkplay.com/

Laugh. Think. Play is a new movement – it is a place that will grow over time – my vision for it is that it is a movement that will change the world. I want to create an app where you can choose what you want to do more of that day. I want people to know and be involved in it as a movement. The why and the how will become clear over the next few years and it is the title of my next book…

SOCIAL MEDIA

LinkedIn:
https://www.linkedin.com/in/emma-stroud

Facebook:
https://www.facebook.com/emmastroudldn/

Twitter:
https://twitter.com/emmastroudldn?lang=en

Instagram:
https://www.instagram.com/emmastroudldn/

Clowning Around Podcast on Instagram:
https://www.instagram.com/clowningaroundpodcast/

Laugh Think Play on Instagram:
https://www.instagram.com/laugh.think.play/

Email:
emma@emmastroud.london

Printed in Great Britain
by Amazon

13193325R00098